Shakespeare's Portrayal
of
The Moral Life

By

FRANK CHAPMAN SHARP, PH.D.

Assistant Professor of Philosophy in the
University of Wisconsin

HASKELL HOUSE PUBLISHERS LTD.

Publishers of Scarce Scholarly Books

NEW YORK. N. Y. 10012

1971

First Published 1902

HASKELL HOUSE PUBLISHERS LTD.
Publishers of Scarce Scholarly Books
280 LAFAYETTE STREET
NEW YORK, N. Y. 10012

Library of Congress Catalog Card Number: 76-121352

Standard Book Number 8383-1069-9

Printed in the United States of America

TO

PROFESSOR CHARLES E. GARMAN

IN GRATITUDE AND AFFECTION

TABLE OF CONTENTS

INTRODUCTION

If conduct be "three-fourths of life," or in other words if all deliberate action have a moral bearing, Shakespeare's description of the moral world is but a name for his collected works. Accordingly, since nothing that is broadly human was foreign to his mind, or failed of at least a passing notice at his hands, the title of the following study would seem to be as comprehensive as that of the professorship founded for Professor Teufelsdröckh at the University of Weiss-nicht-wo. The aim of this undertaking, however, is a modest one. Using as our material the concrete facts of life as they appear in the pages of the great dramas, we shall merely attempt to discover what light they throw upon a single group of ethical problems. Manifestly such an inquiry may be confined within definite limits.

The problems of ethics fall into two distinct classes. First, the moral life of the race as it actually exists and has existed calls for description and explanation. Starting from the phenomena of moral approval and disapproval, in other words, from the fact that certain actions are judged right and others wrong, we here ask: What is the nature of the moral judgment, to what kinds of action does it attach itself, and under what conditions does it arise? Under these few rubrics may be disposed a long series of familiar topics: the standard or standards by which conduct is judged, the nature of conscience and its mode of working, the nature and source of the consciousness of obligation, the conditions under which responsibility is imputed (the ethical side of the free-will controversy), and the relation of metaphysical and theological beliefs to morality. Others closely related, as the connection between character and happiness, and the dynamics of virtue and of crime, will naturally suggest themselves in the course of such an inquiry. In the exploration of this broad field a second set of problems soon presents itself. For the morality that is proves to be a mass of inconsistencies and in part absurdities. Accordingly the question forces itself upon us, How can we reduce the moral judgments of mankind to a consistent and reasonable system, where the word "reasonable" means that which would approve itself to a mind cognizant of and sensitive to all the facts of human experience. The first part of a complete treatise on ethics is thus in method a science, the second an art.

To the catholic mind both of these departments of inquiry are alike interesting and important. Every wise man will accept with gladness any assistance in either direction which the skilled observer of human life is able to offer him. Unfortunately, however, the aid that Shakespeare can give us is limited to the descriptive branch of the subject. Of what he thought about the art of living — and this includes the art of judging — we have no direct and little indirect evidence. There are, indeed, certain historical romances masquerading under the name of biographies that profess to inform us what he thought and how he felt upon almost every subject of human interest. But their results are obtained by picking out from the varied deliverances of his characters those with which the novelist happens to agree. Criticism upon such a method seems superfluous. I at all events shall not attempt to use it. I shall confine myself to an account of the moral life as it is represented upon Shakespeare's stage. I shall treat his characters as if they were living beings, whose consciousness we — happy peepers and botanizers — were permitted to explore. My descriptions, of course, must be in general terms; but the formulæ in which they are presented will be mine, — objective statements, as far as possible, of what I discover in my journey through the world he has created. What thoughts arose in the dramatist's mind as he contemplated his creations thus becomes a matter with which I have nothing to do. Not merely how he criticised but also how he generalized are subjects that alike fall outside the inquiry that is here proposed.

How far these offspring of a poet's imagination resemble the men and women with whom scientific ethics attempts to deal, I have in the main refrained from considering. There is as yet no sufficient concensus of experts in this field to make the subject worth discussing, although we are undoubtedly nearer the goal than we were a generation ago. At only one point has a departure from this plan seemed desirable, namely in the study of moral pathology. The reasons for making an exception in this case will appear in their proper place.

But while questions of truth and error are allowed for the most part to pass unconsidered, the following study is not intended as a mere exercise in literary interpretation. It is an attempt to lay before the reader the results of the observations of a man who was one of the most gifted students of human nature the world has ever seen. The record that he left no worker in the humanities can afford to neglect. No worker, in fact, does neglect it. But the concreteness of its form and the intermixture of irrelevant material — irrelevant from the point of view of science — which is the consequence of the motives that brought it into being, these have operated to render much it could teach us practically non-existent. For this reason it has seemed worth while to re-write that portion which deals with the moral life. In the process its beauty dies and for many people its interest entirely disappears. There may be some, however, who will care to make a systematic review of the materials which the great observer has collected. In this hope the present experiment has been hazarded.

In order to get Shakespeare's powers at their best, I have confined myself as far as possible to those dramas which received their present form after the close of the year 1600, or in other words, to the works of the third and fourth periods according to the common classification. These dramas, it will be remembered, were written during the last ten, or at most twelve years of the poet's literary life, after an apprenticeship, if such we can call it, that had begun, at the very latest, as far back as 1590. It has not, indeed, proved practicable to exclude all references to the earlier works, especially the English histories. But it will be found that, where issues of importance are at stake, it is the four great tragedies, the Roman and Greek histories, the small group of romances, and the so-called comedies, All 's Well that Ends Well, and Measure for Measure, that supply in the main the material for our investigation.

Shakespeare's Portrayal of the Moral Life

CHAPTER I

A STUDY OF MOTIVES

THE fundamental fact of the moral life is the approval and disapproval of conduct. It might therefore be expected that our first topic would be an account of the moral judgments expressly enunciated by Shakespeare's characters. Such indeed would be the prescription of logic. But the nature of the material at our disposal compels us to begin with a study of the motives in which the life of action has its source. True it is not with conduct, but with judgments upon conduct, that ethics as such has to deal, yet no absolute line of demarcation can be drawn between the two. Every action entitled to the name of voluntary is the outcome of a judgment approving it, pronouncing it an action that for some reason, or perhaps for many reasons, it is well to perform. These reasons are the motives. A study of motives is thus a study of the points of view from which conduct may be approved, and a complete enumeration of the motives, persuasive and dissuasive, operating in any given case would, therefore, reveal to us the totality of the grounds on which the judgment of the agent was passed at the moment of action. Any such enumeration might seem to involve a hopeless task on account of the multitude of the threads that enter into the fabric of even the most commonplace life. But by confining our attention to the highest types of moral endeavor we so far narrow the field that it can be explored, while at the same time we omit nothing that is really essential. At the conclusion of our inquiry, we should accordingly expect to be in possession of the data with which to construct a theory of moral judgments.

Our study of motives may fittingly begin with an examination of King Lear, that tremendous drama of struggling optimism in which are disclosed the sublimest heights and deepest abysses of human character. What inspired the humanity of Albany and the devotion of Gloucester, Edgar, and Kent? Let us listen to the confession of that loyal servant who has more than once been pronounced the most perfect character in Shakespeare. The childish old king, thrown into a fit of petulance at the ruin of a pretty little theatrical effect through what he considers the unreasonable obstinacy of one of the actors, has just disowned his best-loved daughter and parted her patrimony between her sisters. Kent attempts for the second time to interpose, when Lear with mounting passion cries:

"Kent, on thy life, no more.
Kent. My life I never held but as a pawn
To wage against thy enemies; nor fear to lose it,
Thy safety being the motive."

Lear I. i. 156.[1]

What made his master's safety his motive? He himself tells us as he enters in disguise the palace from which but a few days before he had been driven as an exile:

"Now, banish'd Kent,
If thou canst serve where thou dost stand condemn'd,
So may it come, thy master, whom thou lovest,
Shall find thee full of labours."

I. iv. 4.

"Thy master whom thou lovest!" This is the key to a devotion which did not ask that master's favor, which survived his prosperity and the integrity of his mind,—a devotion which was no mere selfish clinging to an object of affection as was Antony's passion for Cleopatra, but rather the visible expression of a spirit of self-forgetting service quickened by veneration, love, and pity. In the wild night on the heath, when the dis-

1 The text of all quotations from Shakespeare and the numbering of lines follow the Globe Edition.

guised nobleman and the fool are trying to prevail upon Lear to take refuge in the hovel, the old king turning to his companion plaintively asks, "Wilt break my heart?" Answers Kent: "I had rather
III. iv. 4. break mine own." This is not declamation, it is prophecy. For as soon as the strain was over and his charge had been brought in safety to the French camp, the summons came calling him to his long home. While recounting to
V. iii. 216. Edgar Lear's wanderings "his grief grew puissant, the strings of life began to crack," and he fell tranced to the ground. The warning voice was not misunderstood. Come to bid his king and master aye good-night, he sees that master gently carried before him through the portal. He scarcely notes that with a new ruler a better era is to dawn, for his thought is fixed upon the journey he must shortly go. The end is at hand; and soon, like the faithful fool, he will have "gone to bed at noon."

While in Kent altruism, or the spirit of service, derives its strength primarily from love, in Gloucester we find it awakened by the emotion of pity. "Alack, alack, Edmund," he says to his son after Lear has rushed out into the storm, "I like not this unnatural dealing. When I desired their leave that
III. iii. 1. I might pity him, they took from me the use of mine own house." Soon he is compelled to formulate his motives in the presence of the infuriated daughters and the Duke of Cornwall, for they have been informed by the treacher-

ous Edmund of his final attempt to serve Lear by sending the old king to Cordelia.

Cornwall. Where hast thou sent the king?
Gloucester. To Dover.
Regan. Wherefore to Dover?
. . . .
Gloucester. Because I would not see thy cruel nails
Pluck out his poor old eyes; nor thy fierce sister
In his anointed flesh stick boarish fangs.
The sea, with such a storm as his bare head
In hell-black night endured, would have buoy'd up, **III. vii. 50.**
And quench'd the stelled fires:
Yet, poor old heart, he holp the heavens to rain.
If wolves had at thy gate howl'd that stern time,
Thou shouldst have said "Good porter, turn the key,"
All cruels else subscribed.

Pity, too, is the source of Albany's devotion to the cause of Lear, if we may believe the taunts of his ferocious wife. When at last he has been forced to open his eyes to the true nature of this woman, he turns upon her and tries to blast her with invective. Utterly unmoved she retorts:

"Milk-liver'd man!
That bear'st a cheek for blows, a head for wrongs:
. . . . **IV. ii. 50.**
that not know'st
Fools do those villains pity who are punish'd
Ere they have done their mischief."

Goneril is reproaching him, it will be remembered, for delaying to take the field against the French army which has entered England to restore her father to the throne. Almost the next moment brings her new evidence of the workings of compassion. In the midst of their mutual recriminations a messenger enters bearing the information:

> "The Duke of Cornwall 's dead:
> Slain by his servant, going to put out
> The other eye of Gloucester.
> *Albany.* Gloucester's eyes!
> L. 70. *Messenger.* A servant that he bred, thrill'd with remorse [pity],
> Opposed against the act, bending his sword
> To his great master."

It is to this same emotion that Cordelia's thought spontaneously turns as the natural restraint upon inhuman deeds:

> "Had you not been their father, these white
> IV. vii. 30. flakes
> Had challenged pity of them.

And the hard-hearted Edmund apparently shares her view of the place of this motive in the system of human incentives. For he reminds the soldier
V. iii. 31. sent to kill Cordelia, "to be tender-minded does not become a sword."

A study of the place of love and pity in the other plays would lead to similar results. They are not merely recognized as forces that exist; they are

counted among the most important incitements to
service, the most powerful and widely diffused re-
straints upon selfishness and passion. It Tempest I.
was pity that moved Prospero to teach ii. 353.
Caliban; it was pity to the general wrong of Rome
that drove from the heart of Brutus the J. C. III. i.
pity for his friend; it was pity (or hu- 165–172.
manity) that moved Pisanio to disobey his master's
command to murder Imogen; and this Cym. III. ii.
same humanity that made Camillo at the 15–17.
risk of his life and in the face of certain exile warn
Polixenes of the death prepared for him W. T. III.
by his friend and host. The belief in ii. 166.
the universality and the power of pity is attested by the fact that to it the suppliant habitually addresses his principal appeal; so Arthur in King John, Isabella in Measure for Measure, and Marina in Pericles.

In the preceding description altruism has been represented as aroused by some strong emotion. There is, however, a calm regard for another's good which is capable of moving to action, just as the apprehension of our own good may control our conduct without the intervention of any appreciable feeling. Does Shakespeare recognize and report this fact? The answer is not easy to give. The little that can be said on the subject may best be reserved for another place.[1]

It will now be clear that altruism is represented by Shakespeare as one of the most important factors

[1] See p. 38.

in the moral life. This suggests the question: Do his men and women, after the fashion of some well-known moralists, identify virtue with altruism, or do they recognize the pursuit of what are primarily personal goods to be legitimate or even obligatory? Before attempting an answer, certain possible misunderstandings must be cleared from the way. It has often been asserted that there is no real conflict between altruism and egoism, that your good is my good, because what is for your best interest is for my best interest also. The data upon which this assertion rests do not concern us here; but even if they be permitted to pass unchallenged the conclusion drawn from them involves what has been called the psychologist's fallacy. This form of muddle-headedness consists in the substitution of the point of view of the observer who is acquainted with all the relevant facts for that of the person he is observing. Manifestly if the agent believes himself to be making a sacrifice, a conflict with his egoism may actually take place. Manifestly such a person may ask himself how far the spirit of service ought to be allowed to carry him. Again, it has been urged that self-sacrifice does not represent any assignable phenomenon of human life, that what goes by that name is the identification of my own good with the good of another, the making of his good mine. The substance of this contention must be granted, but there still remains the problem: Within the area of my own good how much consideration ought to be shown for that which is my good solely because it is another's, and that which is mine independently of what the other's interests may be? No analytical subtleties can volatilize into nothingness the world-old struggle with this perplexity.

We accordingly enter upon no barren inquiry when we study the claims of egoism against altruism as conceived by the people of Shakespeare's world. At the outset one fact emerges with unmistakable clearness. The ideals of what is due as between friend and friend, servant and master, benefitted and benefactor, and in general those who stand in some exceptionally close relation to each other, are uniformly set very high. Witness Isabella and Cordelia, Antonio, the merchant of Venice, and Coriolanus, who throws away vengeance and honor at the prayer of his mother. Witness the gruff soldier Enobarbus, who takes his life in remorse at having abandoned a master who had long forfeited all claims to his allegiance. But the obligations to service are not limited to those who can urge special claims. Camillo gives up what he most loves, and risks his life to save the life of Polixenes, a stranger and a foreigner. What he suffered in leaving his native land, a W. T. IV.
self-condemned exile, is shown by the ii. 4–10.
passionate longing he feels to return to Sicily, notwithstanding the brilliant position that his judgment and character had won him at the court of his new master. It is the story of a single noble deed that we read in The Winter's Tale; but

Antonio, Cerimon, and Timon in his palmy days, are represented as passing their entire lives in acts of helpfulness and service. What these men do, they and others approve. For they are not despised by their neighbors as eccentric fools; but rather are they looked up to with humility and reverence, as men born to show their grosser fellows a more excellent way.

Such lives need not betoken, however, a creed of complete self-abnegation. For some at least of the most altruistic characters distinctly recognize the existence of a proper limit to service. The Duke of Vienna, enumerating to Claudio the evils of life, treats as entirely legitimate the pursuit of ends having a purely personal value. In his

M. for M. III. i. 5–41.

arraignment of the fate that ever holds the good before our eyes but forbids us to grasp it with our hands, there is no trace of the dogma enunciated by Fichte: "Whoever thinks of his own interests as an interest at all, and desires any life and being whatever, and any selfish indulgence whatever, save in the race and for the race, he is at bottom, whatever be the good works with which he seeks to hide his misshapen form, nothing but a base, despicable, utterly wicked, and at the same time unhappy man." An explicit assertion of the rights of self occurs during the dispute between Orlando and his older brother in As You Like It. The latter having feigned compliance with the other's demand for an education and an allowance sufficient for his proper support, Orlando replies: "I will no further offend you than becomes me for my good." Still more unequivocal are the words of Rosencrantz to King Claudio: I. i. 83.

"The single and peculiar life is bound,
With all the strength and armour of the mind,
To keep itself from noyance."

Hamlet III. iii. 11.

Rosencrantz is not exactly a member of the moral *élite;* but the force of what he says consists in the fact that it has the air of a commonplace, expressing not merely what people do but what all would admit they ought to do.

The principle stated in the words just quoted is often embodied in action. Isabella, — that spirit so pure that even the foul-mouthed Lucio holds her as a thing ensky'd and sainted, — Isabella declares herself willing to die but not willing to lose her soul in order to save her brother's life. And while this of course does not represent her real motive for refusing the infamous offer of Angelo, it is certainly a consideration that appeals to her as reasonable. The highly idealized Henry V. — "the mirror of all Christian kings" — never thinks of waiving his claim to what has fallen to him and his heirs by gift of heaven, and washes his hands of all responsibility for the bloodshed that will follow the assertion of his right. In leading the English army into France, his point of view is not that the laws M. for M. II. iv. 105–108.

of succession have imposed upon him a duty to others which he must not permit himself to shirk; nor is it that we owe a duty to the world at large to maintain our personal rights, as Ihering insists in his Kampf ums Recht. Henry simply argues as follows: This fruitful land of France is mine; therefore, let the consequences to others be what they may, I am justified in possessing myself of it.

Where, then, lies the limit? The son of Henry's royal opponent, on learning of the English demands, encourages his father to resist with the words: "Self-love is not so vile a sin as self-neglecting." This, however, is no universally accepted axiom. We find Antonio professing himself willing to make any sacrifice, however extreme, for his kinsman Bassanio. And we know his are not empty professions. Desdemona, in like manner, assures Cassio of her readiness to do more for him than she dare for herself. Amidst this diversity of opinion we meet one statement that appears to rest upon a principle which has found a wide, though by no means universal acceptance among moralists. When the Athenian senator is asked for a loan of money with which the most pressing obligations of the now bankrupt Timon may be met, he urges, by way of excuse for refusal, his own extreme necessities, and as major premise asserts: "I must not break my back to heal his finger." In this phrase seems to be implicitly contained the doctrine that has been formulated by

Henry V. II. iv. 74.

Othello III. iv. 130.

Timon of Athens II. i. 24.

Professor Sidgwick as follows: "One is morally bound to regard the good of any other individual as much as one's own, except in so far as we judge it to be less, when impartially viewed, or less certainly knowable or attainable."[1] The fact that this maxim is used by a hypocritical ingrate as an excuse for the cold-hearted treatment of a former benefactor argues nothing against its value. For, as Coleridge has pointed out, some of Shakespeare's worst scoundrels give utterance to the profoundest moral truths. Since no one is represented as deliberately and with foreknowledge breaking his back to heal another's finger, after the manner of Maggie Tulliver, we cannot tell how such a sacrifice would have been regarded. At all events the limits set by this principle are those which the moral tact of Isabella teaches her to respect. When asked by Angelo how much she would do to save the life for which she pleads, the instant reply is: "As much for my poor brother as myself." The doctrine that in cases of conflicting interests duty goes with the greater need can thus claim at least one high-minded and enlightened adherent. **M. for M. IV. iv. 99.**

Which if any of these different views represents the dramatist's own position it is unnecessary to ask, even were it possible to answer. What is of interest is the fact that we find mirrored in Shakespeare's world the chaos of opinion on this subject which prevails in the society by which we are

[1] The Methods of Ethics; Fourth Edition, p. 382.

surrounded, and at the same time a wide-spread recognition that the moral ideal demands a balance, a mean between absolute altruism and absolute egoism.

Great as the emphasis placed upon self-forgetfulness may sometimes be, there is one personal good the desire for which is represented as not merely legitimate under all circumstances, but also as a normal constituent of the ideal character. This good is honor. The Trojan Hector, the English Hotspur, the courtier Camillo, the merchant Antonio, the artless Desdemona, and Cato's heroic daughter, each could say with Brutus: "I love the name of honour more than I fear death." He who is dominated by such a spirit, provided he has at the same time a just sense of what it demands, can do no wrong. "That you would love yourself, and in that love not unconsider'd leave your honour,"[1] is for this reason the point of the petition which Queen Katharine carries to her royal husband in behalf of his oppressed subjects. She believes that if the monarch's sense of honor can be actively enlisted her cause is safe.

Henry VIII. I. ii. 14.

Honor is a somewhat ambiguous term. But the meaning it carries in Shakespeare's plays will appear with perfect clearness if we examine the use of the corresponding verb. This connotes, we find, the two closely allied emotions of admiration and

[1] This passage occurs in a part of the play commonly assigned to Shakespeare.

respect. A sufficient example is the passage in Cymbeline, where the description of the virtues and excellences of Posthumus by one of his friends calls forth the exclamation on the part of his companion, "I honour him even out of your report." I. i. 54. In agreement with this usage, the love of honor will signify either a desire for the respect and admiration of others or a desire for the possession of those elements or traits of character which are the objects of respect and admiration.

In the plays, as in real life, these two closely allied impulses are for the most part inextricably intertwined. Occasionally, however, one is discoverable in separation from the other. It is at honor in the exclusive sense of the admiration of his fellowmen that Falstaff is girding in his famous monologue on the eve of the battle of 1 Hen. IV. Shrewsbury. V. i. 127–143. But while the fat knight will have none of it, the desire for a good name is pictured as a dominant force in every generous nature. Thus Enobarbus, debating whether to remain true to his defeated master Antony, strengthens for the moment his failing loyalty by the reflection

"He that can endure
To follow with allegiance a fall'n lord A. & C. III.
. . . . . xiii. 43.
earns a place i' the story."

Potent as is the desire for the applause accompanying elevation of character, it yields precedence in the highest representatives of the race to the desire for the applauded thing itself. The nature of the spell which character exerts upon the noble mind can be indicated with exactness. For if that quality in virtue of which an object evokes admiration may properly be called beauty, then we may maintain with him of "the pasteboard and the battered hack": "There are two kinds of beauty, the beauty of the body, and the beauty of the soul." To this aspect of the moral life, Shakespeare's people, true children of the Renaissance, were as sensitive as the Greeks. References to actions or to the character behind them as comely, fair, or beautiful, or on the other hand as foul or ugly, recur constantly; and the phrase *καλὸς κἀγαθός* — impressive witness of the completeness with which for the Greek mind the conceptions of the good and the beautiful were interwoven — actually meets us in English dress in the well-known passage from Hamlet:

Hamlet III. iv. 161.

"That monster, custom . . . is angel yet
in this,
That to the use of actions fair and good
He likewise gives a frock or livery,
That aptly is put on."

How literally these epithets may be interpreted is shown to demonstration by the words in which the Duke of Venice dismisses Desdemona's father from the council chamber:

"If virtue no delighted [delight-giving]
beauty lack, Othello I. iii. 290.
Your son-in-law is far more fair than
black."

Here moral and physical beauty are expressly placed in the same category. It is thus thoroughly in keeping with the attitude taken towards character throughout the plays that their one ethical definition should read: "Virtue is beauty." T. N. III. iv. 403.

Beauty of character, like beauty in the realm of nature, discloses itself in varied forms. These we find not merely portrayed — as we should expect, — but also more or less explicitly analyzed. The definition just quoted from Twelfth Night occurs in a passage that begins:

"In nature there 's no blemish but the
mind; III. iv. 401.
None can be call'd deform'd but the unkind."

By "unkind" our philosophical sea-captain means without gratitude or natural affection. Here is a recognition of the fact that the grateful and affectionate mind is directly attractive for its own sake, quite independently of what any one can "get out of it." As such it is fairly entitled to be classed with the beautiful. A study of the eulogies scattered through the plays would show that the virtues of generosity, as in forgiving an enemy, of forbear- Cf. Lear I. iv. 281.

ance from self-assertion, which is a form of the same, and of the broad spirit of self-devotion to the common weal are in like manner valued for their own sakes. By parity of reasoning the adjective noble by which they are designated must be interpreted as possessing an æsthetic connotation.

A second form of moral beauty, — one whose claim to the title no one would think of disputing, — is the display of will-power. Wherever we behold the strength that at need can crush passion and the lust for ease and pleasure, the courage that can face loss without flinching, the fortitude that can bear without a murmur, the patience that can work or wait for an issue long delayed, the energy that breaks down every obstacle, there we feel ourselves in the presence of a power whose least effect demands our homage, and whose higher manifestations bow us down in humility and awe, and make us think we "walk in hallowed cathedrals."

It is obvious that power of will may exist dissociated largely or entirely from affection, gratitude, generosity, or indeed any form of the altruistic spirit. Hence the two principles of beauty that have been described may come into conflict with each other. It is also possible that the spectator of life's drama may be so stunted in mind and heart as to be incapable of responding to the charm of affection and humanity. Naïvely assuming that no one else can possess what he lacks, he will interpret all devotion as the outcome of fear or weakness of some sort, and thus as the mark of a slavish spirit. For such a one there can be nothing great in man but power. This view, propounded long ago by the sophists of the Gorgias and the Republic, has been recently revamped by the German rhapsodist, Nietzsche, and forms the burden of the message which he has felt constrained to bring to a Philistine world. Childish as are many of the dicta of this half-finished personality, preposterous as is his "philosophy" when taken as a statement of the whole truth about man, there is unquestionably a certain grandeur in the ideal which he sets himself to recommend. "Beau comme une tempête, comme un abîme," exclaims Renan of the career of Nietzsche's idol, Cæsar Borgia, and few lovers of the Renaissance would gainsay him. Nevertheless, for the well-rounded mind such admiration is only possible through a certain effort of abstraction. And in proportion as the capacity to see or imagine the man and his actions in their entirety is developed, will repulsion tend to destroy enthusiasm where power appears dissevered from altruism.

Similar changes of appreciation occur where the relation between these two qualities of will is reversed. There are many amiable persons in the world who wish others well but who are incapable of overcoming any serious obstacle in their behalf. When such persons show equal inefficiency in the advancement of their personal interests and are at the same time free from gross passions, their weakness is apt to be regarded by the superficial as at worst a mere peccadillo, at best as an actual addition to their charm. Henry VI. is a representative of this type. Tender-hearted, honorable, sincere, modest, a lover of his country, a partisan of the good cause, he lacks decision, energy, courage, and even pride, — in short, the power to assert himself in the face of opposition. For popular thought, despite these ominous deficiencies, he remains the "saintly king." Nevertheless he cannot escape the condemnation of the judicious. And though his fall may evoke our pity, it is not with us as when we see his noble uncle, the Lord Protector, worthy brother of Henry V., struck down by his enemies in the midst of his life work.

In passing judgments upon character, however, we must not overlook the difference between absent power and latent power. Power can be revealed to its possessor and the world only as it is demanded for overcoming resistance. But there are those so harmoniously constituted that storm and conflict are strangers to their inner life. If this be due to a cowardly retreat in the presence of privation or danger, or to barrenness of the emotional and impulsive nature, the result either inspires contempt or appeals to us as insipid. But where there is great wealth of emotional endowment, a capacity for devotion to the highest ends which, though untried, is not without its witness, there we have a new variety of moral beauty. In distinction from the heroic this may perhaps be called the idyllic.

The keynote of the idyllic life is peace, peace with the world and with self. In such a nature there are no warring passions to be crushed, no temptations to profit at the expense of others to be overcome, while envy, hatred, and malice, that make man the enemy of man, have here no place. The authority of right is owned with glad self-surrender, and in the service of others is found the source of deepest and most permanent joy. To such a one Duty is no stern law-giver, nor does he know her except as a friend.

"There are who ask not if thine eye
Be on them; who in love and truth,
Where no misgiving is, rely
Upon the genial sense of youth;
Glad hearts! without reproach or blot
Who do thy work and know it not."[1]

The idyllic character is in some respects a direct antithesis to the heroic. The hero appears before us with his head surrounded by the halo of victory, but the pain of conflict has left its mark. For this reason, as Schiller has pointed out, the sublime in life always contains an unæsthetic element. But to the child of sunshine and of spring can fall no victor's crown, because he knows no strife. For what the hero accomplishes only at the cost of effort and pain, is for him a work of ease and joy.

[1] Wordsworth: Ode to Duty.

Nevertheless the antithesis is far from complete. In this world of jarring forces, untroubled peace usually comes as the fruit of conquest. On the other hand, there are instances where the soul has known nothing else. Endowed at birth with a temperament that turns to virtue as instinctively as a flower to the sun, that shrinks from the touch of sin as from the defilement of pitch, that knows no distinction between the interests of self and of others, its various impulses are so finely tempered and so exquisitely adjusted to each other that their spontaneous play is goodness. Like the lily of the field it is beautiful without toil, without care, without intention. Even here, however, the principle holds that the suggestion of power must not fail. Think for a moment of Perdita and Miranda, those fair forms that, glorified by all the resources of the poet's art, pass across the scene like visitors from a higher world. Wherein do they surpass a Henry VI.? Is it not in this, that, whereas the latter can never be anything better than a carpet-knight, these two delicate creatures possess a strength and intensity of devotion which, if need arises, will lift them high into the sphere of the heroic?

It is not entirely true, then, that none can be called deformed but the unkind. He who embodies the ideal of goodness must be endowed in equal measure with the spirit of service and power of will. Think of Cordelia; think of Horatio; think of those two great characters that stand at the summit of the creations of the second and fourth periods, Henry V. and Prospero. With an amount of repetition that is unusual, this union of strength and unselfishness is declared to be the very substance of moral perfection:

> "Thou hast affected the fine strains of
> honour,
> To imitate the graces of the gods;
> To tear with thunder the wide cheeks o' the air,
> And yet to charge thy sulphur with a bolt
> That should but rive an oak."

Cor. V. iii. 149; cf. M. of V. IV. i. 184–197; M. for M. II. ii. 107–117; Cym. IV. ii. 169–176.

An age that lends its ear to every new voice will do well to heed this warning directed alike against sentimentalism and the worship of the *Raubmensch.*

The foregoing analysis will exhibit the error that lurks in a now popular doctrine. It is quite generally held that altruism, or the regard for my neighbor's interests, and honor in the sense of the regard for my own character, are but different names for the same thing. This confusion has its source in what has already been referred to as the psychologist's fallacy. Objectively considered, a man with a high sense of honor, guided by proper judgment and an adequate conception of responsibility, will be led by it to the same line of action as the man whose will is set in motion by the awareness of another's needs. It will often come to pass, therefore, that the desires to do ease to another and grace to one's self will be indistinguishable except as the agent happens to be by profession or by nature an analyst. But that the motives are not identical is shown — if in no other way — by the fact that one may act where the other is totally wanting.

Hamlet I. i. 131.

This appears clearly in the career of Banquo, that would-be receiver of stolen goods, who has succeeded in imposing upon a long line of commentators. This canny Scotchman was perfectly indifferent as to what happened to his sovereign, provided his own hands were not soiled in the operation. Like Sextus Pompey in a similar situation he is willing to approve anything, provided he may be kept in ignorance of it until the time for preventing it is past. The only difference is that Pompey forbids his captain to carry out the treachery which would make him master of the civilized world, while in that very moment reproaching the same captain for not doing it without orders; whereas Banquo simply asks that he may not be called upon to take an active part in the foul play which he suspects is being planned. It is quite true that Banquo might have been saved by a more adequate conception of responsibility; he does not seem to have comprehended that a man is answerable not merely for what he does but also for what he can prevent. There is no evidence, however, that Kent was better instructed in the theory of responsibility than was

Antony and Cleopatra II. vii. 67–86.

Banquo; but his thoughts were primarily upon his king, not upon his character; therefore, theories of responsibility were not necessary for him.

What appears to be the same action may thus have its source in one of several different types of character. The representative of the first type is moved habitually by the desire for his own perfection; he may thus act quite correctly though by nature icy cold. His neighbor, on the other hand, may be at times, or habitually, thoughtless of his own perfection. He serves others because he wishes them well. Finally these two sets of motives may be combined in the same individual, as in the case of Brutus. Whether a person shall belong to one class or another will depend partly upon temperament, partly, also, upon circumstances. Some men seem to have been born with a looking-glass before the face. On the other hand, moral self-consciousness may be the result of life in the midst of a corrupt society. It is mainly for this reason, I believe, that Isabella, the heroine of Measure for Measure is so sternly conscious of her virtues. Which of these types is most perfect it may not be necessary to determine. But the clear-sighted student who compares Isabella with Miranda will discover that the effects produced upon the spectator in the two cases are essentially different.

If virtue be beautiful and thus attractive, it should follow that vice is hideous and repulsive. But this is not the whole truth. Certain forms of vice are not merely hateful in so far as they involve qualities the direct antitheses of the corresponding virtues; they possess, in addition, the power of arousing a sort of physical revulsion, direct, unreasoned, but sometimes of unmeasured intensity.

The emphasis laid upon this fact by Shakespeare is a characteristic feature in his delineation of the moral life. The terms employed to describe the feelings are taken by preference from the senses of taste and smell. Iachimo, tossed about by the winds

Cym. I. vi. 47. of lust and shame, cries out, "The cloyed will longs for the garbage." King Claudius, awakening in a moment of remorse to the true nature of his crime, expresses the loathing

Hamlet III. iii. 36. with which it fills him in the words, "O, my offence is rank, it smells to heaven." The climax of Timon's repulsions is expressed in the same terms. Timon of Athens having lavished his wealth upon sycophants and parasites finds himself in the day of his need utterly abandoned by these feeders on his bounty. In the prosecution of a dramatic revenge he invites his false friends to a great feast. Upon the table stand the long rows of dishes as of old. But there is a new

Timon III. vi. 95. tone in the host's invitation to partake: "Uncover, dogs, and lap," he cries. The dishes being uncovered are found to contain nothing but warm water. While the guests look at each other in amazement at this strange scene, Timon seizes the dishes, and throwing the water into their faces, screams in an ecstasy of hatred and detestation:

"This is Timon's last;
Who, stuck and spangled with your flatteries, L. 100.
Washes it off, and sprinkles in your faces
Your reeking villany."

The specific feeling which the use of this imagery is intended to connote is described in express terms by the boy in Henry V. who had accompanied Nym, Bardolph, and Pistol, that graceless trio of braggarts and cut-purses, to the Henry V. III. ii. 55. French wars: "I must leave them and seek some better service: their villany goes against my weak stomach, and therefore I must cast it up." The oft-recurring epithet, "unclean mind," evidently takes its origin from the same area of experience.

We must not suppose that all this is merely vague metaphor, indicating in a general way the dislike which is awakened by every form of immorality. Apart from sporadic cases, like the aversion of Hamlet and the English Tory to marriage with the nearest relatives of a deceased husband or wife, these unreasoned antipathies are called forth by three great classes of actions. The first is weakness of will in its various forms, as cowardice, lack of fortitude, and absence of self-control. These inspire contempt. The second includes all that can be subsumed under the term treachery, as hypocrisy, flattery, and most forms of mendacity.

For the emotion appropriate to them we ought to restore the old word despisal. Finally there are the forms of sensual indulgence such as gluttony, drunkenness, and incest. These arouse the emotion of disgust. It will be found that in the main Shakespeare confines the terms which suggest the nauseating to the second and third groups of vices.

CHAPTER II

TRANSCENDENTALISM

No careful moralist will pretend that the preceding study contains a complete enumeration of the forces which bring into existence and mould into its present form the moral life. However, it includes, I believe, all the material relevant to our purpose that Shakespeare has supplied. Whether the data thus collected are sufficient to serve as the foundation of a structure worth the trouble of building, it is no part of the present design to inquire. But it should be noted that if the sketch just given is substantially correct in the sense that no farther additions would necessitate any radical modifications in the general theory that it would suggest, then its significance lies quite as much in what it omits as in what it contains. Looking upon the compassion of Gloucester and the glowing devotion of Kent, no student of ethical history can forget that for a very important school of moralists all this display of feeling, while doubtless very affecting, is certainly not morality. With Kant, for example, the action, to have moral value, must be performed solely for the sake of obeying the command of reason; everything else is morally worthless. This does not mean that he condemns pity and love as such. He simply asserts that since they involve no attitude whether of obedience or rebellion to the law of reason, the actions to which they lead have no more moral quality than eating at the promptings of hunger.

This view, though familiar enough to the professional moralist, is so remote, I believe, from any conception that would spontaneously suggest itself to the layman that it appears to call for some elucidation.

The phrase "obedience to reason" may mean a variety of things, but for the typical transcendentalist, like Kant or Fichte, it carries the imagination to a world higher and more satisfying than the barren heap of shifting sand upon which is cast our present lot. This supersensible world is conceived to be fundamentally different from our own, and the most orthodox representatives of the school never tire of reiterating that an impenetrable veil hides it completely from our eyes as long as we dwell upon this humble planet. Nevertheless, we can assert that it has its own laws like every well-ordered state, laws which its members unquestioningly and cheerfully obey. Of this mysterious realm we, too, are citizens. For while our lower, or sensual, impulses proclaim our kinship with the brute, our rational nature can only be explained as an emanation from a higher world. We, then, are temporary exiles, or better, colonists sent out to reclaim certain portions of the material universe from the rule of night and chaos. Being citizens of such a commonwealth we are bound to obey its laws, not because they are rules for attaining the most satisfactory life during the few short days of our mission here, but simply because they are the laws of the fatherland, and disobedience reduces man to the level of the animal, the native inhabitant of this world. So a Greek, living for a time among a barbarian people, might refuse to bend the knee before a Persian despot's throne, because it is contrary to the custom of his native city for a free man to prostrate himself before a mere fellow-being. Or he might restrain himself in a fit of passion from killing his slave, not from any motive of humanity, but solely from a consideration of the kind of conduct which in his far-away home is considered becoming in a Greek citizen. In like manner, the sojourner in this world must obey the laws of the land to which he really belongs, or lose his title to citizenship, with the dignity thereto appertaining. The fundamental moral motive is therefore loyalty, born of reverence, to the laws of an invisible state.

Morality thus has primarily and essentially nothing to do with this transitory life of ours and its petty needs and interests. If the course of action which the supersensible law commands happens to coincide with the demands of mundane welfare, or if it turns out to be the fruit into which beauty and strength of character naturally ripen, such an outcome is treated as a mere matter of chance, or at best a pre-established harmony. On the other hand, if this higher law conflicts at any point with the requirements of human welfare, the latter has not the slightest moral claim. Hence the "Fiat justitia, ruat cœlum," and Kant's dictum that the lie of benevolence is never justifiable.

Does the transcendentalist announce these doctrines as conclusions that have gradually forced themselves upon his mind, the significance of duty as a symbol of the supersensuous revealing itself only as he slowly delves into the depths of the moral consciousness? Of the ablest and most consistent members of the school we can answer, no. Kant, for instance, never tires of insisting that no one can be called upon to obey a purely unmeaning command, and such, he holds, would be the moral imperative if the mind knew nothing of its origin and import. He accordingly asserts not once but many times that the common man in his longings for nobility of character places himself in thought in an entirely different order of things from that of his sensual desires. In thinking of himself as the possessor of intrinsic personal worth, he becomes clearly conscious of his position as a member of a higher world, the world of the pure intellect or reason.[1]

Fichte's view is the same in principle, though the statements of the master who had never been a hundred miles from Königsberg are somewhat

[1] See Grundlegung zur Metaphysik der Sitten, Hartenstein Edition, Vol. IV., p. 302; Abbott's translation, p. 74.

toned down by the more cosmopolitan pupil. For Kant "there is no one, not even the most consummate villain, provided only that he is otherwise accustomed to the use of reason" (*i. e.* is not an imbecile), that is blind to the transcendental significance of the moral imperative. Fichte, on the other hand, teaches that while every normally constituted individual is possessed of this consciousness, nevertheless he who habitually yields to his lower impulses may gradually become oblivious of his higher nature till at length it is nothing more to him than the fairy tales of his childhood. "As a man's affections are, so is his knowledge," and "according to what we ourselves are, do we conceive of man and his vocation."[1] Furthermore, a second cause of moral myopia is admitted in the following somewhat enigmatical statement: "[Those] who, besides possessing the natural proneness to mere sensuous activity which is common to us all, have also added to its power by the adoption of similar habits of thought . . . can raise themselves above it, permanently and completely, only by persistent and conclusive thought; otherwise, with the purest moral intentions, they would be continually drawn down again by their understanding, and their whole being would remain a prolonged and insoluble contradiction."[2] Taking into account the tone of Fichte's writings

1 Fichte's Popular Works, translated by Wm. Smith, pp. 319 and 355.

2 *Opus cit.*, p. 369.

as a whole, we may set this class down as either narrow and obtuse, or as obstinate and self-willed, or as warped by the longing for forbidden fruit. In short, the seer of Jena proclaims that his description of the rational world and our relation to it represents nothing beyond the most familiar elements of the every-day thinking of the average man. If you the reader fail to recognize its counterpart in your own experience, that fact merely proves that you are either mentally defective or morally corrupt.

If we are to believe such doctrines as these, the virtues of Shakespeare's characters must be "splendid vices," for no one of them betrays any participation in these gorgeous visions. The Countess, in All 's Well that Ends Well, sends Bertram out into the world rich in her blessing and laden with good counsel; the Duke of Vienna entrusts the reins of government to Angelo in words that bring before him a broad and noble ideal of duty; Volumnia pleads for Rome before her all-conquering son; Brutus debates long before striking down the friend whom he loves and for whose death he must weep; Prospero thrusts back the thoughts of vengeance that rise in his soul; Hamlet covers himself with reproaches for inertness of thought and deed in the presence of obligations the most sacred that his conscience acknowledges; Enobarbus wrestles with temptation, falls, and then, overwhelmed with remorse, makes the only amends still remaining in his power. But the considerations dwelt upon by each of these, apostate or confessor, have nothing to do with any celestial order, and remain exactly what they are, whether such an order exists or not. Says Fichte: "I do not pursue the earthly purpose for its own sake alone, or as a final aim; but only because my true final aim, obedience to the law of conscience, does not present itself to me in this world in any other shape than as the advancement of this end."[1] If any of Shakespeare's characters cherished such a sentiment they were very careful to conceal it. If they attributed it to others, they did not act upon their convictions.

But transcendentalism may be stated in a vaguer and therefore more plausible form. Still defining morality as obedience to reason, and, as before, understanding by reason the faculty of apprehending supermundane laws, it may be admitted that the ultimate source and authority of the command are not necessarily apparent to the common mind. This is revealed only to the student of Kant. What the man on the street knows is merely that certain actions are unreasonable and others reasonable, and that a being who possesses reason ought to obey reason, this knowledge being accompanied by a tendency to obedience. Or, if he does not formulate it thus, he is conscious at least of an impulse to do certain things which are not recommended by any of the motives enumerated in the

[1] *Opus cit.*, p. 374.

last chapter, and which *de facto* have their source in the commands of reason. On the whole the matter is represented thus in the plays of Schiller, notably in Wallenstein, although his account of the inner life of his characters is too incomplete and vague to be intelligible without the help of his systematic writings. While a transcendentalism of this stripe is incompatible with the teachings and spirit of Kant, it may be actually adopted as a modification of his theory.

Does reason thus defined appear as a motive in Shakespeare's works? In general, the term is
e. g. 2 Henry IV. IV. i. 157. there used for the power of apprehending truth. In its application to conduct, it means first the capacity of adjusting means to ends, and secondly the capacity of judging correctly as to the relative value of different ends. The latter is clearly its meaning in the sonnet on lust.

Sonnet 129, lines 6 & 7.

> "Past reason hunted, and no sooner had
> Past reason hated, as a swallow'd bait."

In A Midsummer Night's Dream, again, reason appears as the power of correctly estimating values. Lysander, having under Puck's charm forsaken his yesterday's love, is now pursuing the once-despised Helena with an urgency and a violence which she cannot understand. In answer to the charge of mocking her, Lysander replies with the warmth of the newly baptized proselyte:

"Content with Hermia! No; I do repent
The tedious minutes I with her have spent.
. . . . M. N. D. II. ii. 111.
The will of man is by his reason sway'd;
And reason says you are the worthier maid."

The word judgment is frequently used in the same sense. e. g. Hamlet, III. iv. 70.

It is but a short step from reason as the critic of values to reason as what may be called prudence, that is, the impartial regard for the totality of our personal interests. As such it appears in Iago's disquisition to Roderigo on the power of the will: "If the balance of our lives had not one scale of reason to poise another of sensuality, the blood and baseness of our natures would conduct us to most preposterous conclusions: but we have reason to cool our raging motions, our carnal stings, our unbitted lusts." (Othello I. iii. 330.) In the same strain Enobarbus, while choosing to follow still "the wounded chance of Antony," though others are deserting the defeated triumvir, avows "my reason sits in the wind against me." (A. & C. III. x. 36.)

There are, it is true, some cases which do not fall into any one of the preceding three or four categories. But the number is so small as absolutely to preclude the hypothesis that reason, in the sense in which transcendentalism employs it, is a factor of any importance in the great moral conflicts portrayed in Shakespeare's dramas. Quite apart from their infrequency, their character is such as to afford little aid and comfort to the rationalistic theory, as will appear upon subjecting them to the slightest examination.

Returning to reason as the equivalent of prudence, it will be remembered that its traditional foe is that ill-defined group of emotions and impulses which goes under the name of the passions. Hence it comes about that action determined by reason occasionally stands for the antithesis of action due to the impulsion of passion. Here reason evidently means such motives of whatever sort as act without the assistance of any strong emotion, motives, therefore, which are most likely to obtain a hearing in our calmer hours. An example of this usage will be found in Macbeth, Act II., scene iii., lines 116, 117:

> "The expedition of my violent love
> Outrun the pauser, reason."

Among the motives that are capable of acting without the spur of intense feeling must be counted altruism, the regard for another's welfare. In at least two passages reason seems to be used for such an altruism. The first occurs in Julius Cæsar, where Brutus, dissecting the character of Cæsar says:

J. C. II. i. 20.

> "I have not known when his affections [passions] sway'd
> More than his reason."

The second will be found in the Tempest. Prospero has his enemies in his power, but overcomes the temptation to avenge himself with the thought,

> "Though with their high wrongs I am struck to the quick,
> Yet with my nobler reason 'gainst my fury
> Do I take part."

Tempest V. i. 25.

It must be confessed, however, that both these utterances are somewhat ambiguous.

Only a single passage now remains to be explained. In this the word is used as a generic name for the higher faculties of the mind, intellectual and volitional, as opposed to the sense capacities which we possess in common with the brute. Hamlet, comparing his own apathy in the presence of solemn obligations with the craving for activity which has drawn Fortinbras and his Norwegian followers to fight for a straw upon the plains of Poland, exclaims in one of his characteristic bursts of futile emotion:

> "What is a man,
> If his chief good and market of his time
> Be but to sleep and feed? A beast, no more.
> Sure, he that made us with such large discourse,
> Looking before and after, gave us not
> That capability and god-like reason
> To fust in us unused."

Hamlet IV. iv. 33.

That this avowal of enthusiasm for the exercise of mental power, and of contempt for the life of sloth and sensual indulgence has no necessary connection with the speculations of transcendentalism, will be clear, I believe, from the preceding chapter.

Our conclusion can be summarized in a few words. The theory that defines morality as obedience to reason, where reason means the faculty of apprehending supermundane laws, may be given the name of rationalism. Rationalism thus defined is as little in consonance with the spirit of Shakespeare's plays as is the highly articulated Kantianism of which it is the pale reflection.

A third form of transcendentalism remains to claim our attention. It finds the source of the moral life, not in respect for a law, but in loyalty to a lawgiver. Such a view may, perhaps, be called authoritism. It has been held in somewhat varying forms, its most prominent representatives being the so-called intuitionists. In examining this doctrine we must understand exactly what it affirms. No sane man doubts that for many persons the belief that God commands veracity, respect for property, and much else, is a very powerful factor in securing conformity to the requirements of morality; just as is the command of the sovereign and the parent, in the state and the family, respectively. The real questions in dispute, at least in our own day, are these: Is loyalty to God an unanalyzable element of consciousness, something, therefore, which is irreducible to any motive or combination of motives as yet shown to exist? Is it in nature and origin absolutely unique, something without a parallel among the other constituents of the mental life? Finally, is the loyalty thus conceived the sole source of the consciousness of moral distinctions? The student who has answered these questions to his own satisfaction has defined his attitude towards the common elements of the authoritive theories.

Of these questions the second can be despatched with the most ease. Beyond controversy, in Shakespeare's world loyalty to God is not a unique sentiment without a parallel among mundane springs of action. At every turn the duty we owe God and that which we owe an earthly sovereign are placed side by side, as if identical in nature. Everywhere loyalty to the heavenly and to the earthly king are treated as the same emotion.

Examples are not far to seek. When Norfolk and Bolingbroke are about to meet in mortal combat on the fateful day for which England was to bleed in the War of the Roses, Norfolk, standing armed in the lists, cries out in answer to the marshal's summons:

"[I] hither come engaged by my oath—
Both to defend my loyalty and truth
To God, my king and my succeeding issue,
Against the Duke of Hereford that appeals me;
And, by the grace of God and this mine arm, Richard II. I. iii. 17.
To prove him, in defending of myself,
A traitor to my God, my king, and me."

When King Richard, after forbidding the combat, exiles the principals and compels them to swear eternal enmity to each other, he summons them to take the oath in the following significant language:

> "Lay on our royal sword your banish'd hands;
> L. 179. Swear by the duty that you owe to God —
> Our part therein we banish with yourselves —
> To keep the oath that we administer."

His meaning is: By your banishment you have ceased to be English citizens bound in allegiance to me; there remains, therefore, no anchor for your faithfulness to your word except the allegiance you owe to the Heavenly King. The identity in nature of loyalty to God and king is stated, if possible, still more explicitly in a later scene of the same play. Again the words are Richard's:

> "Revolt our subjects? that we can not mend;
> III. ii. 100. They break their faith to God as well as us."

In Richard II., then, we find a representation of obligation that brings before the mind a picture of a society organized in the spirit of feudalism. At the bottom is the serf or retainer, as the case may be; then the over-lord; then the king; ascending one step higher there is God, in a perfectly literal
Richard III. sense "the great King of kings." The
I. iv. 200. subject owes service to his lord, both

owe service to their common king; all of these owe service to the omnipotent Ruler throned in regions inaccessible to sense. Whatever may be the nature of the loyalty that prompts the subject to submission in each of these relations, it appears to be exactly identical throughout the entire range of its activity. The treatment of loyalty in the other plays, including those of the later periods, is only a repetition of the same tale.

Well, so be it, some one may say, admitted that loyalty to God is not different in kind from loyalty to the king, is loyalty of any sort reducible to motives that we have already studied? Is it not an ultimate, unanalyzable element in human nature? Consider, he may urge, the attitude of the race in the presence of authority. Here is one man out of the millions who dwell within the limits of the fatherland; his commands are obeyed, while the attempt of any one else to exercise such control is either met by a contemptuous refusal, or, if necessary, is repelled by force. Disregarding the influence of fear, affection, suggestion, and other well-known forces whose existence has never been doubted, something still remains to be explained. Surely this residual element is without a parallel among springs of action, is utterly mysterious and even miraculous.

It might seem as if a discussion of this, the fundamental contention of authoritism, were absolutely precluded by the nature of our materials. But unfortunately for him, the Englishman has been driven only too often to reflect upon the nature of political obligation. From the day when Bolingbroke snatched the crown from the hands of Richard II. till the death of Elizabeth, but two English monarchs, Henry VIII. and Edward VI., ruled with the unquestioning consent of their subjects. The others had to defend themselves against rival claimants, many of whom had gained the allegiance of a powerful faction. Thus the thinking Englishman found himself compelled to formulate as best he could his reasons for feeling constrained to yield a subject's obedience, as the only way of determining to whom the obedience was due.

We shall not be surprised when we find these moral conflicts mirrored in the pages of Shakespeare. For through the greater part of Elizabeth's reign her throne rocked on its foundation, and was universally considered even more insecure than events proved it to be. Her title rested primarily upon her legitimate descent from Henry VIII. But when we consider the grounds upon which the king obtained his first divorce, it becomes obvious that either she or her predecessor, Mary, must be a usurper, and consequently the partisans of one or the other, traitors. No orthodox Roman Catholic could admit for an instant the validity of the claim of Anne Boleyn to be a lawful wife and queen; and the Protestant, capable of distinguishing between the use of legal forms by brute force and obedience to the spirit that created them, must have admitted to himself that the position of the mother of his sovereign had been in reality little better than that of an acknowledged mistress. Elizabeth's second title rested upon the will of her father; but can a kingdom be disposed of after the manner of a second-best bed? This was a new problem, involving a principle so remote from previous usage that, by common consent, on the accession of James VI., no attention was paid to the provisions of that same will, which would have given the crown to another branch of the family. Lastly, the third title was grounded upon an act of Parliament. But can Parliament invest with a right to rule one who can urge no other claim? In early English history this question had been answered in the affirmative more than once. Under the Tudors, however, those days were for the most part forgotten, and the generation that crowned Elizabeth's immediate successor was to see such doctrine damned as heresy.

The intelligent citizen of a modern monarchy would base the obligation to obey the command of a fellow-man upon the principle that the kingly office is a public trust, and the king simply the first servant of the state. He looks upon the law of hereditary succession as "nothing more than an expedient in government founded in wisdom and tending to public utility" — to use the words of an eminent English judge of the eighteenth century.[1]

[1] Sir Michael Foster, in Taswell-Longmead English Constitutional History, p. 171, note 5.

With him the motive for obedience is, at its best, that enthusiasm for the common good which in the inevitable cases of conflict leads to the subordination of the individual will.

At first sight such a man seems to have no counterpart in the Shakespearean world. Take, for example, the tetralogy that goes by the several names of Richard II., first and second Henry IV., and Henry V.[1] Richard II. is represented, in agreement with the testimony of history, as a thoroughly vicious and at the same time lamentably weak ruler. None of the functions of government was performed properly; life was not safe; the property of the nobles was pillaged, and the merchants were oppressed by means of forced loans, blanks, and, according to the play, benevolences or "gifts" to the crown. In consequence of these things Holinshed, the chronicler who supplied Shakespeare with his facts, looks upon Richard's deposition as a righteous act, and apparently the public utility doctrine would permit no other attitude. Yet the best characters in the play look upon Bolingbroke's coronation as a monstrous crime. The Bishop of Carlisle, a man of patriotism and honesty, risks his life in a protest flung into the teeth of the newly created king. What is more striking the leaders of the rebellion, Northumberland and Bolingbroke, admit in after years the immorality of their course. True, Nor-

[1] The view that these plays are essentially one need not carry with it any implications as to the dates at which the several parts were written.

thumberland's confessions of guilt appear as the product of his newly conceived hatred for his present master and of a desire for another change. Nevertheless his expressions of self-reprobation do not sound like mere pretexts; they seem to represent rather the outcome of sober second thought, clarified, no doubt, by disillusionment. Surely there can be no question of this fact in the case of his son, Hotspur. And whatever we may think of the Percy family, nothing can have a more genuine ring than the dying declaration of Henry IV.:

> "God knows, my son,
> By what by-paths and indirect crook'd ways
> I met this crown.
> . . . . . .
> What in me was purchased [*i. e.*, stolen],
> Falls upon thee in a more fairer sort;
> So thou the garland wear'st successively."

2 Henry IV. IV. v. 184 ff., 200 ff.

The effect produced upon the hearer or reader by these confessions is heightened through the employment of contrast, a favorite device of the dramatist. The quarrel between Norfolk and Bolingbroke, upon which turns the plot of Richard II., had its origin in the murder, or alleged murder, of the Duke of Gloucester, uncle of both Richard and Bolingbroke. The agent was Norfolk, but behind him was supposed to have stood the king himself. One of the earliest scenes of the play represents the good Duke of York, a brother of Gloucester, hounded on by the widowed duchess to revenge himself upon his royal nephew. The old man is far from insensible to her appeal, but his loyalty stands firm as a granite cliff.

Richard II. I. ii. 37.

> "God's is the quarrel; for God's substitute
> Hath caused his death: the which if wrongfully,
> Let heaven revenge; for I may never lift
> An angry arm against His minister."

Here we may see how the good man acts when the criminal that wrongs him is his sovereign.

And yet there is another side. The noble and enlightened Henry V., the ideal man of action, though the son of a self-confessed usurper, has no scruples about his own title to the throne. He knows it will be attacked, and he intends to defend it. It is only his weak and sentimental son, Henry VI., with his double incapacity for seeing fact and dealing with fact, that displays any anxiety on that score. Furthermore in King John, written apparently about the same time as Richard II., we find the best intellect and character arrayed on the side of the "usurper."

No one can misunderstand the function of Faulconbridge in this play. He is to be taken as the representative Englishman. Keen of insight, sane of judgment, noble in heart despite his whimsical outbreaks of self-slander, he clearly stands for the

best thought and most scrupulous conscientiousness that the times could show. It will be remembered that John is represented as basing his claim to the crown solely on the pretence that Arthur, the supposed son of his elder brother, Geffrey, is in reality illegitimate. There is no element of historical truth in this picture, for England in the thirteenth century was in fact, as in name, an elective monarchy. John's title, based on his election by Parliament, was consequently all that he could desire. Nevertheless, the play, as we have it, knows nothing of the Parliamentary prerogative. We may gather from certain words that escape Faulconbridge in a moment of passion, that he does not attach the slightest value to the **John IV.**
story of Arthur's illegitimacy. Yet he **iii. 142–145.**
never, for an instant, considers joining the French army that has been set in motion to restore the unfortunate young prince to the throne. On the contrary, his loyalty and devotion to his master seem as great before Arthur's death as after the boy's fatal leap from the castle wall, when, according to the strictest theory of primogeniture, John became the rightful sovereign. Just as little is he influenced by the wickedness and misgovernment of the king. In the conflict between John and the English barons who, after the death of Arthur, offered the throne to Louis of France, on the ground of John's moral unfitness for the office, Faulconbridge is the mainstay of the royal party.

The solution of these apparent paradoxes is not

far to seek. Let us remember that the miseries and the anarchy of the reign of Stephen had been caused directly by a struggle over a disputed succession; that the French Philip, who was posing as the champion of the "legitimate heir," Arthur, was at bottom seeking to make England an appanage to a foreign throne; let us further remember that the Bishop of Carlisle is permitted to see, in prophetic vision, what was still fresh in the minds of Elizabeth's subjects, the disorders of the reign of Henry IV., and the horrors of the War of the Roses, an enormous price even for deliverance from the rule of a profligate tyrant; let us remember these things and we shall see that to side with John against the "legitimate heir," and to side with the despotic Richard against the stronger, wiser, and, in reality, nobler Bolingbroke, might be the policy of the same man, one, namely, whose grounds of action were throughout a consideration of what was likely to be most conducive to the permanent welfare of his country.

Richard II. IV. i. 136–149.

The outcome, then, seems to be clear. Shakespeare represents civic loyalty, where it is most open-eyed and unselfish, as a form of patriotism. And the principle of allegiance that is recognized in practice by his noblest and most intelligent men is one which as formulated by the theorist would read: The right to the throne and the right to demand obedience when on the throne are neither inexplicable nor absolute; their ultimate source lies in their relation to the public good. Henry V. explicitly acknowledges the validity of this principle. When, on the eve of his departure from France, he discovers the plot that has been formed to kill him, he feels that the wrong done him is in a high degree a personal one, for one of the conspirators is his best-loved friend. As a man he nevertheless forgives them, and would gladly spare their lives. But as one called upon to consider his kingdom's safety, he is obliged to overrule his personal wishes, and therefore as king, in the interest of the common weal, he condemns them to death.

Henry V. II. ii. 166–181.

Should it be urged that the welfare theory of sovereignty is, at most, latent in the historical plays, and that the language and actions of their characters are explicable in other ways, the reply can be made that in any event the theory is formulated with the greatest clearness in one of the maturest products of the poet's genius.

The great play of Coriolanus is not an attack on "the people," as is often imagined, for the mistakes and sins of the title hero are far more serious than those set down to the account of the Roman mob. It is rather a study in the workings of political forces. Written at a time when Parliament was awakening from its long lethargy and was beginning to assert the political rights of the people as a whole, the play describes the beginnings of the conflict between the Roman aristocracy and the masses which, after dragging on for five long centuries, was to end with the establishment of Cæsarism. The last steps in this drama had already been traced in Julius Cæsar, and Antony and Cleopatra.

At the moment of the opening of Coriolanus the people have just won a notable victory. They have obtained their first bit of political power in the shape of the creation of the tribunate. From first to last Coriolanus is the consistent and bitter opponent of this concession on the part of the patricians. His reasons are stated with a clearness that leaves no room for misunderstanding, a force with which no character in the play seems able to cope, and a completeness which in another writer would have converted the play into a didactic treatise. He fears for the consequences of the first grant because, extorted as it is by force, he believes it will inevitably lead to farther concessions. Then when this has grown and there are two powers in the state, neither supreme, he foresees the destruction of good government, then anarchy, and finally, enslavement by some foreign power. The only safety lies in the rule of a small homogeneous body with unrestricted power, wise, provident, and capable of leadership. From this principle, and from this alone, he deduces the right to command and the duty to obey.

Cor. I. i. 221 ff.; cf. III. i. 132 ff.

III. i. passim.

III. iii. 127 ff.

III. i.; cf. T. & C. I. iii. 75-137.

It must be added, however, that distinct traces of another mode of thought are occasionally discoverable. For instance, in Henry V., Act I., we find the king of England, together with his legal and his moral guides, examining the claims of the House of Lancaster to the French throne. The point of view throughout seems to be that sovereignty is a piece of property and the king is the owner of his people. On this view, if accepted without reservation and worked through consistently, the crown is like any other possession and carries with it the right of using and misusing. Whatever limitations are placed on these rights can be based solely upon a consideration of the interests of the heirs. For the subject to refuse obedience to a command is a wrong of the same nature as if one person should seek to wrest from another his land or his slaves. The only casuistical questions that can arise with regard to the right to rule, are those relating to the conditions of succession.

It is easy to see the facts which lend plausibility and indeed a certain justification to this view. The kingly office carries with it great emoluments, and the opportunity for earning a reward for service may be considered a right as much as the undisturbed possession of a piece of property. Do not modern law courts seek to protect the manufacturer and the merchant from discriminations that would rob them of their customers? Have not the trade unions issued a new commandment: "Thou shalt not take thy neighbor's job"? That in applying the principle to the relation of governor and governed, its restricted validity should be frequently overlooked is only what might be antecedently expected. This attitude towards sovereignty, therefore, is but an exaggerated outgrowth of loyalty to the institution of property. Of course it may be asserted that respect for property, alone of all the elements of human life, has its origin in motives or faculties inexplicable except by reference to a supersensible world. Such an assertion Shakespeare will not enable us to contradict, for he makes no attempt to analyze either the institution itself or the nature of its claims to our allegiance. As a matter of fact, however, no moralist has had the temerity to take such a position.

If, then, God be strictly representable as the over-lord of earthly kings, we have a clear picture of the relation in which He stands to His subjects. First, His motives for asserting and enforcing His authority become obvious and intelligible. For if Henry V. in his capacity as king denounces murder and treachery because they are harmful, there are no grounds for supposing that the great King of kings commands, "thou shalt do no murder" for any other reason. Secondly, we can understand the motives that prompt Shakespeare's characters to subordinate their will to the divine commands. Apart from fear and love, which are explicitly referred to, and the factor of suggestion, which is not mentioned, we find the conception, sometimes

Richard III. I. iv. 200-202.

formulated, sometimes implied, that God's commandments represent what best conduces to the common good; perhaps, also, some trace of the notion that we are God's possession. The appeal made by the former consideration requires nothing farther for its explanation than public spirit and a desire for one's own sake for security and order. The second idea gets its practical effectiveness from that respect for property which, that we might not be carried beyond our prescribed limits, has been left unanalyzed. In view of all these facts, loyalty, whether to king or God, can urge no claim to be an utterly mysterious and quasi-miraculous motive. It has its source in springs of action that are well understood; it has its source in springs of action whose origin requires no supernatural explanation, except, indeed, in so far as the whole nature of man is divine; it has its source, furthermore, in springs of action that urge men to assume right relations with their fellows quite apart from any thought of a supersensible world.

We have now the answers for the first two questions raised by the doctrine of authoritism. The third and last, it may be remembered, dealt with the relation between loyalty and the consciousness of moral distinctions. The contention of the school with regard to this relationship may be formulated in two statements. First, the apprehension of a certain action as right is identical with the consciousness of an obligation to perform it. Second, the consciousness of an obligation to perform an action arises only in consequence of a belief that it has been demanded by God. Right and wrong being thus meaningless terms, except as the individual turns his face towards his divine King, obedience to Him becomes not a part, but the whole of morality. Accordingly when we say we owe fair dealing or assistance to our neighbor, the truth of the matter is that we owe it to Him to treat our neighbor in that particular way. In other words, the only actions that have moral value are those performed from the motive of loyalty to God.

Whatever may be the objective validity of the above view it could never have been suggested by a study of Shakespeare's characters. In their lives loyalty to God appears simply as one of the many elements that form the substance of the moral life. It does not even claim any sort of preeminence above the rest. No unprejudiced person would pretend that Lear is anything else than a representation of the conflict between the powers of good and evil — one of the most tremendous and awe-inspiring that the imagination of man has ever conceived. Yet the attitude of the nobler combatants towards crime and moral heroism alike is not determined in its essentials by the relation in which they suppose themselves to stand to any supersensible power. Cordelia, when she hears from Kent's lips the story of her father's wrongs, cries out, "Let pity not be believed!" Albany discloses to Goneril his feel-

Lear IV. iii. 31.

ings towards her and his opinion of her outrages in the words:

> "See thyself, devil!
> Proper deformity seems not in the fiend **IV. ii. 59.**
> So horrid as in woman."

These two utterances taken together represent completely the effects of the horrors in the drama upon the conscience of those who saw them. Will any one have the temerity to assert that in reality these men and women had no conscience, that their emotions were merely pathological, as Kant would call them? They at all events called the conflict raging about them a moral conflict. Their emotions of abhorrence or enthusiasm were what they understood by sympathy for virtue, reprobation for vice.

> "O thou good Kent, how shall I live and work, **IV. vii. 1.**
> To match thy goodness?"

exclaims Cordelia. And when the end has come, Albany, now in supreme control, summons to his side Edgar and Kent:

> "You, to your rights;
> With boot, and such addition as your honours
> Have more than merited. All friends shall taste **V. iii. 300.**
> The wages of their virtue, and all foes
> The cup of their deservings."

The German critic Kreyssig has called King Lear the drama of Kant's Categorical Imperative. If by this is meant a presentation of the springs of moral life, such as transcendentalism in any of its forms would recognize, he might as well call Paradise Lost the epic of Darwin's Natural Selection.

In this respect King Lear is an epitome of Shakespeare's world. Much has been said about the absence of religious life in the plays. The fact is, the great majority of the leading characters exhibit in one way or another a belief in the fundamental postulates of religion. On the other hand, their attitude towards God seldom appears as a direct factor in determining their relation to their fellow-men. This statement is so far from holding merely for the criminal and the vicious, that its most complete exemplification is found in the noblest lives. In fact in the Shakespearean drama but two virtues are habitually brought under the special protection of heaven: resistance to the temptations of suicide and of perjury. The reason for these exceptions is obvious: these temptations are oftentimes at once so subtle and so overwhelming that considerations of humanity and honor tend to crumble before them. But even here, if the latter are exceptionally strong, the appeal to the supersensible is not needed.

Consider for a moment the significance of the scene at the meeting of the conspirators in Julius Cæsar. Cassius has demanded that they bind themselves together with an oath. To Brutus such a proceeding seems a blackening of their own characters. If the evils of the times and shame at our fallen estate are not sufficient motives, let us slink, every man to his own home, and give up the attempt to lead the life of free citizens. But Brutus, you object, was an impractical idealist. That is true; but his idealism consisted, so far as this particular case is concerned, in judging others by himself. How far his confidence would have led him astray does not concern us, for we are dealing with the ethical question: How explain a Brutus? not with the statistical one: How many Brutuses are there?

The last contention of authoritism thus falls to the ground. Other actions, we discover, besides disobedience to God, are regarded as wrong in themselves; actions performed without any thought of obedience may be approved as right.

This conclusion apparently leaves on our hands a serious difficulty. For it will naturally be asked how, on such a view, we can explain that feeling of restraint which, when it appears amid the stress of moral conflict, we call the sense of obligation. The logical consequence of the preceding analysis is to place the source of the entire moral life in desires. But a desire is a mental state whose motive power resides in the attraction that is exercised by a proposed end. How can constraint arise out of attraction? Whether this problem can claim a place in a study like the present will depend upon our right to make a certain assumption. If we may believe that Shakespeare described all the elementary phenomena of the moral life, it certainly belongs here; otherwise not. For the consciousness of obligation, in the sense of a feeling of restraint, or indeed in any other sense, appears neither as a fundamental nor an independent factor in any moral experience that he describes; the forces that do battle for the right seem to be, without exception, ideas of a state, whether of self or another, which the agent desires to bring about. We are therefore reduced to two alternatives. Either an important or perhaps the most important constituent of the moral consciousness has been ignored, or else we really have before us all the fundamentals, and the sense of restraint is but a secondary phenomenon which may arise out of the conflict of desires.

Those who accept the latter alternative are bound to point out where and under what conditions this feeling arises. That, in reality, is not a difficult task. A desire will give rise to the feeling of restraint when the actions necessary for its realization come into conflict with strong passions, deep-seated habits, or are otherwise disagreeable in the doing; when, during the action or even in facing the possibility of performing it, we feel as if we were acting along the line of the greatest resistance. In these cases we shrink back and at the same time feel ourselves attracted onward. Thereupon, alike whether we press forward or turn aside, a feeling of coercion or restraint will arise, and, as long as the opposing forces keep their hold upon the attention, will continue.

An illustration of this principle may be found in the tragedy of Hamlet's life. Hamlet possesses a certain ideal of character embodied in his friend Horatio. Its warp and woof are loyalty and the power to pursue one's own way independently alike of every stimulus or distraction that fortune happens to throw into the way. (*Vide* Act III., scene ii., lines 59–79. Note that "just" means loyal.) Such loyalty, according to a code that Hamlet never questions, demands the revenge of his father's murder. Such constancy must he possess if he is to attain success. For the stab of a dagger will not of itself suffice; he must so act as to remain free from the suspicion of selfish motives in the eyes of his mother, his betrothed, and his countrymen. This involves a carefully thought-out and perhaps complicated plan tenaciously followed from stage to stage, till his end is finally gained. But it is just such a course of which temperament and habit have made him incapable. Dependent as he is upon stimuli from without for anything more exacting than idle reverie, he cannot even set his mind to work upon mapping out a coherent plan of procedure. Yet all this time an ideal of strength and devotion is beckoning him onward. Hence it is only with a sense of constraint at moments intolerable that he can give himself up to the life of aimless floating with the current which finally proves his ruin.

In this way it does not seem difficult to explain the feeling of obligation as rooted and grounded in desire or approbation. Whether this or any other account of the phenomenon ever entered Shakespeare's mind, no one who knows what evidence means would pretend to decide. But assuming always that his descriptions are correct, and at least in outline complete, it appears to be the only account compatible with his delineation of the moral life.

Our study in moral dynamics leaves in our hands a principle of the greatest practical importance. If Shakespeare portrays human life aright, morality stands whatever view we may take of the nature of the universe or of the origin and ultimate destiny of man. Let the great heart of things be what it will, we recognize a duty to ourselves, our neighbor, and the general weal, and we have within us powers that respond to their call. Metaphysical and theological belief may strengthen the moral muscle in many ways, but is not its creator. Nor in the completely developed man would there be anything left for it to do. In fact our study of Shakespeare's writings ought to teach us to reverse the traditional view on these matters. The nature of a man's religion, *i. e.*, his relations with God, depends primarily upon his character, though interaction is, of course, not excluded. King Claudius, for instance, was the pink of orthodoxy, and even Falstaff believed — and trembled. But the relation of these men to God, in so far as He had any place in their lives, was a mere matter of buying and selling. Indeed this is the only attitude toward Him that an ignoble mind can take. If, then, the commands of the great King are really to exercise moral restraint of a high order, there must first exist a spirit of self-forgetting service — "He that loveth not his brother whom he hath seen, how can he love God whom he hath not seen?" — or failing this, a desire for the approbation of a companion mind. Morality is thus the creation, not of religious belief, but of ideals without which religion itself could arouse neither reverence nor moral enthusiasm.

CHAPTER III

THE CRITERION OF RIGHT AND WRONG

IN making our way through this jungle of motives I trust we have not forgotten that our aim was to discover the sources of the moral judgment. Every motive, as was pointed out in the beginning of Chapter I., is a ground of approval. Accordingly among the sum total of the motives for the best actions must be found the grounds upon which the agent bases his moral approval of such actions. Taking the agent as a representative of the race, we are thus supplied with valuable material for testing the current theories of the moral judgment.

The clearest and most certain outcome of our exploration is a negative one. Conduct is not approved, primarily, because it is believed to be demanded by a law that comes from a supersensible order and that has no relation to the welfare of human beings in this life. But a positive conclusion seems also warranted. Our analysis of human activities has acquainted us with a class of forces which can be described as interest in the various forms of welfare. And we have found in what every one would agree to call the higher actions such interests to be the dominant motive. We may therefore infer that moral judgments have their source in ideals of welfare; that conduct is an object of moral approbation or disapprobation according to the relation in which it stands to the well-being of self and others. The theory that thus emerges may be called idealism or eudæmonism.

Two easily distinguishable grounds of approval have also been discovered. Kent, we remember, declares that his motive for interposing between Cordelia and the wrath of her father is the latter's safety. This evidently signifies that he approves the action in question because of its conduciveness to an end lying outside of itself, namely, Lear's welfare. Accordingly we seem entitled to assert the existence of moral judgments in which conduct is pronounced right because a means to welfare. Such judgments may be called utilitarian. On the other hand, the point of view in Volumnia's appeal to Coriolanus to spare his native city is of an entirely different nature.

"Thou hast affected the fine strains of
 honour,
To imitate the graces of the gods.
. . . .
Think'st thou it honourable for a noble
 man
Still [always] to remember wrongs?"

Coriolanus V. iii. 149.

The ground for approving forgiveness of enemies is that forgiveness is admirable. Here we seem to have a second variety of the moral judgment, in which conduct is pronounced right quite apart from any thoughts of its ulterior effects, simply because of its own intrinsic excellence. Judgments based upon admiration for beauty in the world of conduct, and immediate antipathy for the ugly, the base, and the vile, may be called æsthetic.

Our confidence in the validity of these conclusions will be strengthened by a study of those cases where circumstances have compelled an explicit formulation of the reasons for which an action is pronounced right or wrong. I pass over such scenes as the night in the garden, when Brutus justifies the assassination of his best friend on the ground that one must

J. C. II. i. 32.

> "Think him as a serpent's egg
> Which, hatch'd, would, as his kind, grow mischievous."

No one would care to base a theory on passages of this kind, because they are too isolated. Two varieties of judgments, however, recur so frequently in the same form that of their nature and significance there can be no reasonable doubt. The first of these is the attitude assumed towards punishment for crime; the second, the approval of the "forced lie."

The casuistry of punishment can be disposed of in a few words. Isabella, interceding for her brother's life, pleads, when argument proves unavailing, "Yet show some pity." Angelo replies.

"I show it most of all when I show justice;
For then I pity those I do not know,
Which a dismiss'd offence would after gall."

M. for M. II. ii. 99.

On precisely this ground, with explicit disavowal of any other justification, Henry V. condemns to death the noblemen who had plotted to kill him. Not the clamors of revenge, not the demands of some abstract conception of justice, but the requirements of the public good, this it is, in his view, that justifies the state in bringing evil upon the evil-doer.

Henry V. II. ii. 174–177.

The principle that right and wrong are determined by a consideration of the demands of the welfare of those directly and indirectly affected, appears likewise in the treatment of veracity. Isabella, suing for the life of her brother before the deputy Angelo, in the supposed absence of the reigning duke, has been offered the boon she begs, on condition that she yield herself to his will. Never for an instant does she think of consenting, and Claudio seems to be lost. But the omniscient friar, who later proves to be the duke in disguise, evolves a well-contrived plan for the young man's rescue. He seeks out Isabella and proposes that she appear to yield, and then send in her stead to the place assigned Angelo's betrothed, Mariana of the moated grange. This unfortunate woman had long ago been heartlessly abandoned by the deputy, but with the tenacity of her sex she had never ceased to love him. "By this," explains the friar, "is your brother saved, your honour untainted, the poor Mariana advantaged, and the corrupt deputy scaled. . . . If you think well to carry this as you may, the doubleness of the benefit defends the deceit from reproof." There is not a moment's hesitation. "The image of it gives me content already," cries Isabella, and prepares herself for her part.

M. for M. III. i. 263.

The farther task of unmasking Angelo necessitates more lies, and here, the stakes not being so great, the protests of the antipathetic emotions make themselves heard.

> *Isabella.* To speak so indirectly I am loath:
> I would say the truth; . . .
> . . . Yet I am advised to do it;
> He says, to veil full purpose.

IV. vi. 1.

Nevertheless, her loathness does not prevent her from carrying out to the letter the instructions that she has been given. In the presence of the duke, who has resumed his state, the dignitaries of the city, and the people who have thronged to witness the entry of their ruler, she deliberately asserts that upon the deputy's demand she allowed her sisterly compassion to confute her honor. The significance of these scenes lies in the fact that Isabella is no weak or compliant mind. She is a woman in whom purity of purpose is the fundamental necessity of life; a woman whose conscience is so sensitive and withal so powerful that she seems to the world "a thing ensky'd and sainted."

Some persons make a difference between lying for their own benefit and that of others; not so Shakespeare's characters. Think, for instance, of the heroine of All's Well that Ends Well, a character superior in beauty even to the statuesque Isabella. Fleeing in the guise of a pilgrim from France to Italy, in order that the husband who hates her may be at liberty to return to his home, she reaches Florence as evening is about to fall. She finds the people of the city congregated outside the walls watching the triumphal entry of their army, just returned from a campaign against Siena. Among the crowd is the landlady of an inn where pilgrims were wont to lodge. With an eye to her professional duties this good woman accosts Helena and engages her to remain all night at her house. Thereupon the usual shower of questions begins:

Widow. You came, I think, from France?
Helena. I did so.
Widow. Here you shall see a countryman of yours
That has done worthy service.
Helena. His name, I pray you.
Diana. The Count Rousillon: know you such a one?
Helena. But by the ear, that hears most nobly of him:
His face I know not.

All 's Well III. v. 49.

Of course Helena could not reveal what that name, so idly spoken, meant to her. She could not be expected to tell what might lead to the discovery that the Count Rousillon was her husband. But had she been a stickler for veracity, after Kant's own heart, she would either have refused to enter upon a course which was, itself, a continuous piece of deception, or, if she could succeed in making a distinction between the spoken and the acted lie, she would have from the first resolved to choose silence where the truth would mean the defeat of her purpose. To be sure, such a procedure might in this case have aroused a curiosity as dangerous as a complete avowal; but then, what of it? If we, as rational beings, are under obligation to make our words a reflection of our thoughts, regardless of consequences, then must she submit to discovery. Helena, however, has other ideas of duty. Too high-minded to shuffle or equivocate, she deliberately makes a statement that she knows is completely false. Like Imogen in Cymbeline, she evidently believes

"If I do lie and do
No harm by it, though the gods hear, I hope
They 'll pardon it."

Cymbeline IV. ii. 377.

Only Helena's conscience demands no excuses.

In the entire range of Shakespeare's plays there is but a single record of a genuine conflict between the impulse to speak the truth, at whatever cost, and the desire to dissemble for what, apart from the deception, would be recognized as a worthy purpose. Coriolanus, having ruined his cause with the people by his plainness of speech, is urged by his friends to return to the Forum and disown his insulting epithets. At first he cannot bring himself to consent. But the ground of his refusal is no more an objection to deceit as such, than it is a regard for the social value of veracity. It is solely the aversion of the proud patrician to the humiliation of bending his uncovered head before the despised mob, of admitting to himself and to them that he dare not say what he pleases. His mother understands him perfectly. Determined that he shall yield, her last move is to appeal to his love for her, the appeal that had never failed. If he will be deaf to that, **Coriolanus III. ii.**

"Come all to ruin; let
Thy mother rather feel thy pride than fear
Thy dangerous stoutness, for I mock at
death **III. ii. 125.**
With as big heart as thou. Do as thou list.
Thy valiantness was mine, thou suck'dst it
from me,
But owe thy pride thyself."

Coriolanus has within him the spirit of the Spartan prisoners who, rather than bear the name of slaves, took their lives. Like the mediæval knight, the lie was disgraceful in his eyes primarily, if not solely, because the sign of a cowardly spirit.

Whether the lies of Isabella and Helena were really justifiable it would be quite irrelevant to my present purpose to inquire. What I desire to show is the manner in which many minds, and those often of the purest intentions, deal with the problem when it is forced upon them. The preceding sketch shows that at least a portion of Shakespeare's world, a portion including some of its highest representatives, more or less clearly conceive the obligation to veracity as dependent upon the needs of social life.

On the other hand, Shakespeare was, of course, well aware that these questions are often decided by other criteria, although for some reason, perhaps because such modes of judgment did not have his sympathy, they do not appear prominently in his writings. Nevertheless, traces of them are not wholly wanting. Thus as we have seen, the duty of the state to requite evil with evil is always based upon the requirements of public welfare. In virtue, apparently of the same principle, private punishment is usually condemned. Vengeance, however, is occasionally counted a sacred duty, as by Hamlet. Similarly with untruthfulness. It is invariably excused where it is supposed to be harmless. But we are occasionally given brief glimpses of another attitude. For instance, when Isabella declares, "to speak so indirectly I am loath," her repugnance does not seem to arise from a computation of consequences.

It is such immediate judgments as these — naïvely

supposed to be common to all men, or at least to all good and intelligent men — that have enabled non-eudæmonistic theories to assert the absence of all essential relation between morality and mundane good. Intuitionism, which it will be remembered is a form of transcendentalism, goes still farther. It interprets the stirrings of resentment, the antipathy to treachery and sensuality, the warming of the heart at the spectacle of courage, as quasi-miraculous intimations from a supersensible world, specific directions or commands as to the manner in which the citizens of that world ought to comport themselves during their enforced sojourn in Vanity Fair. But just as our study of casuistry has shown that not all good and intelligent persons regard these "intimations" as absolutely binding, so our study of motives should have taught us that even in those whom they most completely dominate they exist in the form of ideals. When there is an immediate demand that the wicked be punished, it is due to the desire that the object of our indignation shall suffer; when there is an unreflective horror of the lie, loyalty to truth means purity of character; when Hamlet asks

"Whether 'tis nobler in the mind to suffer
The slings and arrows of outrageous fortune,
Or to take arms against a sea of troubles,
And by opposing end them?"

Hamlet III. i. 56.

there stands before his inner eye the ideal of a strong immovable will. Where a single ideal rules in its own field without a rival, what it demands will be called right. Where no one is supreme, doubt and conflict must arise, and the outcome will be determined — whether we are distinctly aware of it or not — by our view of the relative importance of the interests at stake. Indeed one of the most far-reaching single explanations of the diversity of moral judgments is found in just this difference of opinion as to the relative value of incompatible ends.

The assertion that our actual moral judgments are invariably determined by some conception of welfare may seem to be audacious in the face of the explicit denials of a large body of non-eudæmonistic writers. Does not the transcendentalist, it will be asked, describe the workings of at least his own moral consciousness? Did not Kant and Fichte get their moral code from sources absolutely unrelated to their desires and aversions? The solution of this difficulty is found in the difference that may exist between what we believe and what we believe we believe; or, as Mr. Bosanquet has phrased it,[1] between moral ideas and ideas about morality.

Unfortunately for the progress of ethics the general tendency has been for the philosopher to make

[1] International Journal of Ethics, I., 86 ff. Reprinted in Civilization of Christendom, p. 178 ff.

his doctrines too exclusively a mere reflection of the more salient features of his own moral experience, to the neglect of much he might have learned from the inner life of his fellow-men. But even where self has been the most exclusive object of study, an almost incredible divergence between the standards actually used and the account offered of these standards is demonstrable. Of course this assertion cannot be proved here for the more elaborate doctrines of modern philosophy, but the briefest study of the ethical theories alluded to by Shakespeare's characters will show what is possible in that direction.

Of the three or four of these theories the most popular is that which defines right as agreement with the intentions of nature. Ever since this curious doctrine was explicitly formulated by the Greek sophist, Hippias, about four hundred years before Christ, it has maintained a place in the language and perhaps the thought of men. The demand for a "life according to nature" and the doctrine of "natural rights" represent merely two of its many forms. Among Shakespeare's people the theory comes to light in such phrases as "Nature craves all dues be render'd to their owners," revenge, "that food which nature loathes," and in the words with which the English ambassador demands from the King of France the surrender of his title and his lands. The king, he announces, wills

T. and C. II. ii. 173

Timon V. iv. 32.

"That you divest yourself, and lay apart
The borrow'd glories that by gift of heaven,
By law of nature and of nations, 'long
To him and to his heirs."

Henry V. II. iv. 77.

In vain, however, do we seek for an instance in which Henry V. or any one else consults the "intentions of nature" with regard to matters whose legitimacy he has no other ground to question. One of the most evident intentions of nature is that the masculine half of the race should be distinguished from the better half by the presence of a beard; but the whim having fastened itself upon the men of Europe to assign that function to short hair, we shave and have our hair cut in calm indifference to what "nature craves." Shakespeare's men seem to have felt no more qualms on the subject than we do. So far may our formulæ for our judgments be removed from the veritable grounds on which they are based.

CHAPTER IV

THE NATURE OF THE GOOD

THE foundations of the moral world, we have learned, are laid in the desire for the welfare of self and others. But the term welfare is as vague as an aphorism from Meister Eckhart, and the moralist is bound to make it more definite. Without some conception of its meaning we could not form the simplest decision. Without an exact formula we may be left stranded at a critical period in our career upon the sands of doubt and hesitation, or we may be driven from our course by the blind forces of temperament or swept away by some current of education or fashion. Isabella, for instance, hates a lie; on the other hand, she desires her brother's life. Of two goods the world has room for but one. Let her choice fall as it may, it must assume the truth of some theory of values. To be sure, a formula for the good cannot by itself serve as a pilot to guide us through the intricacies of casuistry, but, supplemented by a correct view of the relation that should be maintained between the pursuit of individual good and the good of others, it is a chart to tell us in what direction our harbor lies.

The good (*bonum*) means, of course, that which is desirable or worth having. In ethical discussions, unless the contrary is expressly stated, it denotes that which is desirable not as a means to an end, but as an end in itself. Among the prominent claimants for the honor of occupying this position are pleasure, activity, breadth and variety of experience,[1] power, the beautiful, knowledge, virtue, and the development of our faculties. The first and the last are the two most prominent candidates, the last under the name of self-realization having been for a considerable period the favorite in the most exclusive philosophical circles. And if within the last few years its popularity has suffered something of a decline, it can still, like a retired political "sage," count upon the devoted loyalty of a faithful few and the Platonic veneration of a multitude of former worshipers.

At the very outset of any inquiry into the nature of the good a formidable difficulty arises. What is meant by the term valuable? It has often been thought sufficient to answer: That is valuable which is desired; that is intrinsically valuable which is desired for its own sake. This definition cannot be called false, for somewhere within the circle of the desired the good must lie. But whether it is adequate is quite another matter. For reasons which will appear in their place I

[1] Cf. Faust: What all mankind of pain and of enjoyment
May taste, with them to taste be my employment.
Faust, part 1, Act II., scene vi. Translation of J. S. Blackie.

shall not, however, follow up this interesting and important question. The majority of the investigators in this field have contented themselves with presenting a formula which they claim will cover all the ultimate objects of desire. The limits of our subject matter will restrict us to an examination of certain of these conclusions.

If by self-realization is meant the developing and perfecting of all our powers and capacities of intellect, taste, and will, then after what has been said in a previous chapter no proof is needed that it fills a large place as a motive in the lives of the broadest and most gifted men. It is true that our study was confined to the will. Yet obviously an interest in the development of all sides of our nature will be the usual accompaniment of a scrupulous care for the perfection of any one of them. A Prospero, therefore, who in the world of action takes the side of his nobler reason against his lower passions will also care supremely for the bettering of his mind. And the frequently expressed ideal of living above the brutes will be found to involve a desire, not merely for emancipation from the power of blind and transient impulses, but also for the possession of every capacity, intellectual, emotional, and volitional, that distinguishes man from the lower animals.

Whether self-realization is entitled to the rank of an ultimate end is a question that we may waive for the moment. However the answer may fall, we may easily assure ourselves that it is not the only object of desire, even in the highest representatives of the race. This will appear from a study of one of the most characteristic features of Shakespeare's world, namely the desire for fame.

To the rôle played by this masterful passion reference has already been made.[1] We meet it at the very beginning of one of the earliest comedies:

L. L. L. I. i. 1. "Fame, that all hunt after in their lives."

From that time on there is scarcely a play where the desire either for fame or its brother, good reputation, is not an important factor in the working out of the plot. Those to whom it means most hold it "far more precious-dear than life," even where life has everything to offer. (T. and C. V. iii. 27.)

The same is true of the closely allied end, good reputation. When Bolingbroke, who is one day to be crowned Henry IV., charges the Duke of Norfolk with treason in the presence of King Richard II., the accused nobleman demands the privilege of clearing himself by the arbitrament of battle. Richard, knowing that he is the real object of Bolingbroke's attack, at first refuses to permit the combat. Thereupon Norfolk breaks forth in words that may fairly be called the fundamental article in the creed of chivalry:

[1] See above p. 15.

"The purest treasure mortal times afford
Is spotless reputation: that away,
Men are but gilded loam or painted clay.
. . . . .
Mine honour is my life; both grow in one;
Take honour from me, and my life is done."

Richard II. I. i. 177.

To stand well with those about us is here declared to be the chief end of man. This language cannot be interpreted as merely the exaggeration of passion, or as a mask of duplicity assumed to conceal the features of crime. For what a man is appears, if anywhere, in his last hours, and the dying thought of some of Shakespeare's noblest characters, — Antonio, Brutus, Hamlet, — concerns itself with the portrait they are to leave behind them in the memory of men.

The significance for our purposes of this attitude towards fame and reputation lies in the fact that both are here valued, not as means to some ulterior end, but as ends in themselves. First, they do not derive their value from any relation to self-realization. This is obvious from their very nature. Self-realization has to do with what we are, or, if you prefer, with the way we appear to ourselves; fame and reputation, with the way we appear to others. To confound things so different is to widen your definition till self-realization means: Whatever I choose to consider a good.

The independence of these two ends is, furthermore, demonstrable by examples. One of the most interesting passages to be found in the entire range of Shakespeare's works is the controversy between the sons of Priam, in Troilus and Cressida. In the seventh year of the war, the Greeks offered to depart forever without demanding any indemnity for their losses, provided the Trojans would give up Helen. The proposition is brought in due form before a family council where at first all favor its acceptance, save Priam's youngest son, Troilus, and naturally enough, his brother Paris. The discussion grows heated, Troilus being the centre of attack. Finally Hector proceeds to define his position for the last time. "The reasons you allege," he says in reply to Paris and Troilus,

> "do more conduce
> **T. and C. II. ii. 168.** To the hot passion of distemper'd blood
> Than to make up a free determination
> 'Twixt right and wrong."

Then follows a solemn assertion of the wickedness of detaining Helen, concluding in an elevated strain:

> "These moral laws
> Of nature and of nations speak aloud
> **L. 184.** To have her back return'd: thus to persist
> In doing wrong extenuates not wrong,
> But makes it much more heavy."

Every one is accordingly prepared to hear Hector insist anew upon the acceptance of the Greek proposals. Imagine their surprise when in the very next breath he continues:

"Hector's opinion
Is this in way of truth; yet ne'ertheless,
My spritely brethren, I propend to you
In resolution to keep Helen still, L. 188.
For 't is a cause that hath no mean dependance
Upon our joint and several dignities."

What can he mean? Troilus understands him instantly:

"Why, there you touch'd the life of our design:
Were it not glory that we more affected
Than the performance of our heaving spleens,
I would not wish a drop of Trojan blood
Spent more in her defence. But, worthy Hector,
She is a theme of honour and renown,
A spur to valiant and magnanimous deeds, L. 194.
Whose present courage may beat down our foes,
And fame in time to come canonize us;
For, I presume, brave Hector would not lose
So rich advantage of a promised glory
As smiles upon the forehead of this action
For the wide world's revenue.

Hect. I am yours,
You valiant offspring of great Priamus."

Here, then, is an indubitable instance of a preference for fame before character, and that by men upon whose idealization Shakespeare has lavished all the wealth of his powers.

The theory of values here implied is explicitly stated (though according to his custom never acted upon) by Hamlet in the soliloquy after his meeting with the fame-seeking Fortinbras. It is put still more strongly in Pericles. In this play the order of dependence affirmed by the perfectionist is deliberately reversed, and virtue and wisdom are declared to be valuable because they assure their possessor an imperishable dwelling-place in the minds of men.

Hamlet IV. iv. 46 ff.

Cerimon. I hold it ever,
Virtue and cunning were endowments greater
Than nobleness and riches: careless heirs
May the two latter darken and expend;
But immortality attends the former,
Making a man a god.

Pericles III. ii. 26.

Of course this is merely Cerimon's polite way of parrying his friends' praise. Nevertheless, to be effective, what he says cannot seem either to speaker or hearers utterly absurd. While, therefore, it need not have been taken by any of them for the whole truth, it must have seemed valid to them as far as it went. In fact, with a little care in selecting one's illustrations, a plausible argument could be made for the position that fame, including, of course, reputation, is regarded in Shakespeare's world as the sole ultimate good.

But if fame is not desired as a means to self-realization, just as little is it ordinarily desired because of the pleasure its attainment promises to afford. A test case is supplied by Cassius, and possibly Brutus, who wished for fame after death, although they did not look forward to a life beyond the grave. Hardly had Cæsar fallen under the blows of the conspirators, when the thought of the leaders, beset though they were on all sides by confusion and danger, turned as automatically as a deflected needle to the glory promised them by their deed.

Cassius. Stoop, then, and wash. How
many ages hence
Shall this our lofty scene be acted over
In states unborn and accents yet unknown!

Brutus. How many times shall Cæsar J. C. III.
bleed in sport, i. 111.
That now on Pompey's basis lies along
No worthier than the dust!

Cassius. So oft as that shall be,
So often shall the knot of us be call'd
The men that gave their country liberty.

Yet Cassius was an Epicurean,[1] and V. i. 77.
Brutus seems to have shared with his IV. iii.
brother Stoics of that day the belief 145.

[1] So also in Plutarch.

that the consciousness of good and evil ends with death. At least, in the farewell between him and his friend we find no reference to the possibility of a meeting in another world. Evidently their desire for posthumous fame was not aroused by the idea of enjoying its realization.

V. i. 115 ff.

Mighty as is the desire for fame, it may yield in potency to the passion of love. Othello was once altogether such a one as Hector; the free active life of the soldier, with its promise of power and renown, the preservation of his reputation for courage, honor, and leadership, these were all in all to him. But the time came when Desdemona became a part of his life. Then in the agony of the supposed annihilation of her affection, he found he could have endured the wreck of his ambition, yes, even the scorn of man, better than the loss of love. Why? At all events not because it meant loss of an important means of self-realization. The love of woman he had never expected, but when Desdemona wept at the story of the dangers he had passed, he needs must love her. And when she had become his wife, his bliss in possession did not arise from the reflection that now a very important and hitherto neglected side of his nature could obtain its development, that his character would become more perfectly rounded and more harmonious as time went on through the growth of latent capacities. No, it is what he has, not

Othello IV. ii. 47 ff.

what he may become that fills his soul with absolute content.

> "If it were now to die,
> 'Twere now to be most happy; for, I fear,
> My soul hath her content so absolute II. i. 191.
> That not another comfort like to this
> Succeeds in unknown fate."

This brief survey seems to me to demonstrate the existence of ends which are pursued for their own sakes, alike without reference to their power of developing faculties, and to the amount of pleasure or freedom from pain they promise to furnish. In view of the present state of ethical controversy, it seems worth while to establish this principle for that important end of human endeavor, the good of others.

"What is your will? That [Lysimachus] have his." The simple and common phenomenon represented in this brief dialogue has been the occasion of many an inky battle. Taken in their obvious signification its words are declared by some to stand for an impossibility. When I act most "unselfishly" my will is really aiming, they imagine, at some state of myself that can be reached only as my neighbor attains the object of his desire. This state may then be described, according to taste, either as sympathetic pleasure in another's success, or as the development of some of my various powers or capacities. Pericles V. i. 5.

The first of these hypotheses appears in a well-known Lincoln story. "Mr. Lincoln once remarked to a fellow-passenger on an old-time mud-coach" — so runs one version of the tale — "that all men were prompted by selfishness in doing good. His fellow-passenger was antagonizing his position, when they were passing over a corduroy bridge that spanned a slough. As they crossed this bridge they espied an old razor-backed sow on the bank making a terrible noise because her pigs had got into the slough and were in danger of drowning. As the old coach began to climb the hill Mr. Lincoln called out, 'Driver, can't you stop just a moment?' Then Mr. Lincoln jumped out, ran back, and lifted the little pigs out of the mud and water and placed them on the bank. When he returned, his companion remarked: 'Now, Abe, where does selfishness come in on this little episode?' 'Why, bless your soul, Ed, that was the very essence of selfishness. I should have had no peace of mind all day had I gone on and left that suffering old sow worrying over those pigs. I did it to get peace of mind, don't you see?'"[1]

That Mr. Lincoln has supplied a correct explanation of many an action there can be no doubt. That the explanation is inadequate to account for all the facts is equally certain. Clarence, brother of Edward IV. and Richard III., warned by a

[1] Quoted from the Springfield (Ill.) Monitor, in the Outlook, Vol. LVI, p. 1059.

dream that the hour of his death is at hand, cries out in agony of soul,

"O God! if my deep prayers cannot
appease thee,
But thou wilt be avenged on my misdeeds,
Yet execute thy wrath in me alone,
O, spare my guiltless wife and my poor
children!"

Richard III. I. iv. 69.

His petition is not for ease of mind about his family, but for his family. He is as far from begging to be assured of their welfare as he is from begging to be allowed to witness it. The direct object of his desire is their good. In fact, the Lincoln paradox is susceptible of a very simple explanation. Unsatisfied desire may become the object of a secondary desire, the desire to be rid of the desiring state. But obviously the secondary desire is made possible by the existence of a primary desire with a different object.

According to the second of the above mentioned hypotheses, when I am making a sacrifice for the benefit of another — as the untutored mind naïvely calls it — I am in reality interested solely in developing my own courage, my power of enduring pain or privation, my sympathies, or some such thing. To put it plainly and without circumlocution, I am merely using my fellow men as material on which to work up my emotional and volitional muscle, a sort of moral Swedish horse or flying trapeze. A man like Kent becomes in this view an exceptionally determined athlete, bearing the same relation to the average mortal that the climber of Alpine peaks does to the business man who gets all the exercise he wants by walking to and from his street-car. This theory is ruled out of court, if put forward as an all-sufficient description of altruistic action, in case we can find an instance of a desire for the good of those whose welfare we cannot affect by our actions, and who therefore make no demand upon the exercise of our faculties. The scene just cited supplies such an instance. When a man who is looking death in the face prays, "O, spare my guiltless wife and my poor children!" he is begging for that which can never affect the state of his moral muscle, one way or the other.

If we may affirm that neither pleasure nor self-realization is the sole object of desire, we must assert with equal emphasis that neither can be excluded from the category of the desired. For self-realization Shakespeare hardly affords us the test case we might expect to have; but surely we are entitled to infer that if a man may desire for its own sake to present a certain appearance to others, he may desire in an exactly similar manner to present that same appearance to himself; or, in other words, if he may desire to seem, he may desire to be.

With regard to pleasure the facts are really beyond controversy. The claims of psychological hedonism have indeed been met by the counter-claim that pleasure is never a direct object of desire nor pain of aversion. But this statement is simply an illustration of the principle that narrowness enkindles narrowness. No one, of course, ever desires "mere pleasure," for there is no such thing. But to say we desire pleasure means that we desire a state because and in so far as it promises to be pleasant. Evidence that this is possible for aversion from pain seems to be afforded by Othello's last words to Desdemona:

> "Not dead? not yet quite dead?
> I that am cruel am yet merciful;
> I would not have thee linger in thy pain."

Othello V. ii. 85.

There may be those who imagine that Othello is merely afraid his mercifulness will lose something of its delicacy if he is not careful to prevent unnecessary suffering. But I venture to affirm that for the spectator not mad with too much learning the tragic power of these brief lines lies in the assumption that at the last supreme moment Othello desires the good of her he still must love, and that he does not regard a prolongation of the death agony by a few minutes or even seconds too trifling a matter to be worthy of consideration.

That the aversion to certain emotional states may be due to their painfulness is exhibited in the plays with even greater clearness. Constance, the widow of King John's older brother, has just lost her only son, and is racked with the agony of a desolated mother. Doubtless she would not be free from her grief at the price of less sensitiveness; that would conflict with an ideal of motherhood which she could not cast away. But if she could be free without lowering herself in her own eyes how gladly would she welcome the change.

> "I am not mad: I would to heaven I were!
> For then, 'tis like I should forget myself:
> O, if I could, what grief should I forget!
> Preach some philosophy to make me mad,
> And thou shalt be canonized, cardinal."

King John. III. iv. 48.

Shakespeare wrote this as a young man. But in the maturity of his powers he portrays a similar situation met in the same spirit. The speaker is the blind Gloucester.

> "The king is mad: how stiff is my vile sense,
> That I stand up, and have ingenious feeling
> Of my huge sorrows! Better I were distract:
> So should my thoughts be sever'd from my griefs,
> And woes by wrong imaginations lose
> The knowledge of themselves."

Lear IV. vi. 286.

The conclusion to be derived from the foregoing analysis is that if good be defined as the object of desire Shakespeare represents a world in which no one formula can be made to cover the content of the idea. Fortinbras, Prince of Norway, risks all for glory; to another man reputation is a bubble. Desdemona would not have been such a woman as Othello thinks her for all the world; Emilia, on the other hand, while she would not choose such a course for a small matter like a ring, is certain she would do it for the world, and she knows many women like herself. Kent thinks that death has been kind to Lear:

> "He hates him much
> That would upon the rack of this tough world
> Stretch him out longer." **Lear V. iii. 313.**

Not so, the thorough-going perfectionist would say. Lear is now restored in mind. Though feeble in body, with, at most, but a few years of life before him, he has still unrealized powers and capacities which are capable of development. That he has not altogether stiffened into the immobility of age is shown by the fact that, in the few weeks of mingled passion and madness since his abdication, the old king has become a different man. When the storm has cleared we find a new light has dawned upon his soul, a light that the sun of prosperity could never throw. Hence he has still everything to live for. True, death has robbed him of his one remaining joy. Drearily, henceforward, will his days drag themselves toward the inevitable end. But pleasure and pain are matters of no importance. Moreover, Cordelia's death, under the circumstances in which it took place, may be expected to bring out new and interesting phases of his character. He hates him much that would see his journey towards perfection shortened by a single step.

Whose judgment of values is correct? Or is there no standard that applies to all men? Is my good simply that which I desire; and when choice is necessary, is the better that which I desire more? We remember Hamlet's answer to this question. Hamlet finds Denmark a prison; Rosencrantz finds it otherwise.

Hamlet II. ii. 255.

> *Hamlet.* Why, then, 't is none to you; for there is nothing either good or bad,[1] but thinking makes it so.

But Shakespeare, who can speak against the thing he says, gives us another view in a passage that may have been written about the same time. During the controversy between the sons of Priam already referred to, the youthful Troilus ventures the same paradox about a woman:

T. & C. II. ii. 52.

> "What is aught, but as 't is valued?"

[1] Not "right or wrong," as this is often understood to mean.

To this Hector at once replies:

> "But value dwells not in particular will;
> It holds his estimate and dignity
> As well wherein 't is precious of itself
> As in the prizer."

In other words, a man's own preferences are not necessarily the sole ultimate standard in determining his good.

Which of the foregoing statements is correct is obviously a problem upon the solution of which all subsequent investigation into the content of the good must depend. Material bearing directly upon it is not, I think, offered by Shakespeare; those phases of the mental life that alone could supply the necessary data, he has not cared to represent. While our results are thus in the main negative, they are not, I trust, for that reason profitless. We have discovered that those psychologists and moralists are in error who describe the will as always directed to a single goal; and we have discovered that, contrary to the assertion of various writers, perfection, pleasure, and the good of others, as well as much else, may become the direct object of desire. These doctrines are not merely of importance in themselves, they derive an added significance from the fact that they represent the only results of the long controversy about the *bonum* that can lay any claim to the dignity of established truths. For they alone, amidst the clash of contending opinions, have been able to secure the allegiance of an ever-increasing proportion of the best contemporary authorities. They may therefore be looked upon as the foundation for all that the future will accomplish in this field of investigation.

CHAPTER V

CONSCIENCE AND THE CONSCIENCELESS

If the great master of those who know human life has succeeded in describing adequately the conflict within the will between the better and the worse, he has supplied the data for defining the fundamental word in the ethical vocabulary. According to certain moralists, as we have seen, conscience is a mystic oracle within the breast through which are transmitted to this lower world the laws of a supersensible commonwealth. According to others, conscience cannot be a separate faculty, functioning by itself in some corner of the mind; it is the mind as a whole regarded as the source of moral judgments. It is in the latter way, if our previous conclusions are warranted, that the matter should be described by Shakespeare. Whether he does in fact so describe it may be determined by studying a typical representation of the revival of moral sensibility.

The scene is laid in the chamber of Queen Gertrude, in the castle of Elsinore. Behind the arras lies the slain Polonius. Turning away with unconcern from the deed his hand has just committed, Hamlet addresses himself to his trembling mother:

"Leave wringing of your hands: peace! sit you down,
Hamlet III. iv. 34. And let me wring your heart; for so I shall,
If it be made of penetrable stuff."

Before them on the arras stands the figure of the murdered king; next to him the man that robbed him of place, of love, of life.

"Look here, upon this picture, and on this,
The counterfeit presentment of two brothers.
See, what a grace was seated on this brow;
Hyperion's curls; the front of Jove himself;
An eye like Mars, to threaten and command;
L. 53. A station like the herald Mercury
New-lighted on a heaven-kissing hill;
A combination and a form indeed,
Where every god did seem to set his seal,
To give the world assurance of a man:
This was your husband. Look you now, what follows:
Here is your husband; like a mildew'd ear,
Blasting his wholesome brother."

How could she turn away from one so noble? How could she forget solemnly contracted vows to throw herself into the arms of "a murderer and a villain;

a slave that is not twentieth part the tithe of [her] precedent lord?" He finds but one answer: the capriciousness of lust. This it is that made her fall a prey to the guilty advances of her husband's brother; that drove from her mind the image of her former lord before he was laid in the grave; that sealed her eyes to the murder of her husband and hurried her into an incestuous union with the murderer. Licentiousness, shallowness of heart, disloyalty to the dead, incest, this is the count. As black on black the picture is painted before her eyes, the better impulses of that fallen nature are quickened into life and the power returns to see herself as she is. "O Hamlet, speak no more," she cries in the agony of self-recognition,

"Thou turns't mine eyes into my very soul;
And there I see such black and grained spots **L. 88.**
As will not leave their tinct."

Love and pity, sorrow and shame at the downfall of her nobler self, loathing for the self that now dwells in its place, these Hamlet has aroused. If the scene is meant to represent the awakening of conscience, these are conscience.

But if, when the situation demands the sacrifice of some personal interest, there be neither altruism in its heaven-directed or earth-directed form, nor desire for perfection of character, nor direct abhorrence of vice, to what can we appeal? Nothing. We may, of course, use bribery or threats; but the result is not genuine morality. The man is conscienceless, whatever he does or refrains from doing. He feels no scruples about the proposed crime and no real remorse for it when past. Shakespeare has not hesitated to draw several such characters. If we disregard Aaron, in Titus Andronicus, on the ground of disputed authorship, his first essay in this direction was Richard III.[1]

To descant upon the crimes of this intrepid villain were to harp upon a hackneyed theme. As every one admits, no traces of moral principle can be discovered in his career as represented in the main body of the drama. In cold blood he plans and perpetrates a series of revolting murders, and feels nothing but satisfaction in his success. But in his last hours, it is often held, this moral indifference disappears. When, on the eve of the battle of Bosworth Field, he is warned by voices whose prophetic nature he cannot doubt that his life is at an end, and when on the black curtain of the night the vision of the past is thrown, scene after scene, then what he calls conscience rises to afflict him. He awakes in terror, while cold fearful drops stand on his trembling flesh.

What are the thoughts that oppress and terrify his soul? It is easy to discover, for to the unbiased observer they are unequivocally revealed. Listen to the cry with which he awakes:

[1] The Shakespearean authorship of Richard III. has been denied by James Russell Lowell, but, it would appear, on insufficient evidence.

"Give me another horse: bind up my wounds.
Have mercy, Jesu! — Soft! I did but dream.
Methought the souls of all that I had murder'd
Came to my tent; and every one did threat
To-morrow's vengeance on the head of Richard."

Richard III. V. iii. 177, 178, 204-206.

From the priest's lips he had often heard that

"The great King of kings
Hath in the tables of his law commanded
That thou shalt do no murder."

L. iv. 200.

That God "holds vengeance in His hands," was a fundamental tenet of his church. Why should he doubt it? There is no evidence that he was a skeptic. In the presence of his generals he could, indeed, scoff at the thought of future retribution:

L. 204.

"Let not our babbling dreams affright our souls:
Conscience is but a word that cowards use,
Devised at first to keep the strong in awe:
Our strong arms be our conscience, swords our law."

V. iii. 308.

But manifestly he is here whistling to keep up his own and his followers' courage. Can he for a moment imagine that God will fail to keep His word? Does he not know that Richard, King of England, has never permitted the slightest act of disobedience to his commands to go unpunished? So with all his bravado he cannot help believing these midnight apparitions to be messengers of divine wrath. For belief in dreams was an unquestioned element in the creed of the time, and what these dreams announced was a punishment that he knew was inevitable, sooner or later. In the heyday of life he could forget the threatening vengeance, but now it is immediately upon him; the vengeance is to-morrow's, and vengeance means not merely defeat and failure, but death and hell. Well may he start in terror, though no coward. But in all this there is no trace of self-condemnation; only fear.

V. iii. 179. "O coward conscience, how dost thou afflict me!"

"O Ratcliff, I fear, I fear,—

Rat. Nay, good my lord, be not afraid of shadows.

K. Rich. By the apostle Paul, shadows to-night

L. 214. Have struck more terror to the soul of Richard

Than can the substance of ten thousand soldiers

Armed in proof, and led by shallow Richmond."

Such fear by itself means no more than that frail mortality believes itself in the hands of Omnipotence, enraged because for the moment its will has been blocked.

But the text as handed down to us contains other matter.

> "What do I fear? myself? there's none
> else by:
> Richard loves Richard; that is, I am I.
> Is there a murderer here? No. Yes, I
> am:
> Then fly. What, from myself? Great
> reason why: L. 182.
> Lest I revenge. What, myself upon my-
> self?
> Alack, I love myself. Wherefore? for
> any good
> That I myself have done unto myself?
> O, no! alas, I rather hate myself
> For hateful deeds committed by my-
> self!"

and so forth, for nine more dreary lines. What are we to make of such words? Is Shakespeare representing this cold-blooded monster as feeling genuine remorse for crime? Can he be supposed to hate himself? Does he intend we shall believe Richard was oppressed with a consciousness of guilt?

The answer to this question involves a problem of textual criticism. "Some parts of [this soliloquy]," says Hudson[1] "are in or near the poet's

[1] Shakespeare: His Life, Art, and Characters, Vol. II., p. 168.

best style, others in his worst. . . . [The latter are] made up of forced conceits and affectations, such as nature utterly refuses to own. . . . It is hard to believe that Shakespeare could have written [them] at any time of his life, or that the speaker was meant to be in earnest in twisting such riddles; but he was. Some have, indeed, claimed to see a reason for the thing in the speaker's state of mind; but this view is to my thinking quite upset by the better parts of the same speech." Now it is noticeable that just those lines of the monologue that are æsthetically painful are ethically perplexing. We have, therefore, our choice between two hypotheses. Either Shakespeare, like Coleridge, in that monstrosity known as Remorse, supposed that sorrow for a misspent life, horror of crime, and self-loathing, can arise in a nature that possesses neither sympathy, honor, nor antipathy for treachery; or — the second alternative — some one to us unknown, thinking this representation of the guilty sinner on the eve of death was not sufficiently accurate, or edifying, or blood-curdling, attempted to improve upon Shakespeare's art by supplementing his deficiencies.

The latter hypothesis is far from gratuitous. "It seems almost certain," says Karl Elze[1] "that [Shakespeare's own manuscripts] never were in a printer's hands, except the manuscript of his Venus and Adonis and his Lucrece which he pub-

[1] William Shakespeare. English Translation, by L. Dora Schmitz, p 296.

lished himself." For this reason and many other equally good ones, textual critics are generally agreed that no one of the plays has come down to us exactly as it was written. If with these facts in mind we compare the lines in question with others that are undoubted interpolations, as Measure for Measure, Act III., scene ii., lines 275–296, and King Lear, Act III., scene ii., lines 80–95, we shall recognize them as the productions of kindred souls. Accordingly the choice seems an easy one. The passage is not from Shakespeare's hand.

But if, soaked with *a priori* ideas of what the criminal ought to feel, we reject this conclusion; if we think it more likely that the youthful Shakespeare wrote doggerel than that he represented a villain living and dying without remorse, we may turn to the studies in crime of the maturer man, the man who in the days of the great tragedies had attained the fulness of his mental stature. The conclusions derivable from an analysis of the characters of Goneril and Iago depend upon no excision of doubtful passages, upon no interpretations that may be forced upon single words or isolated sentences.

It has been said even by keen critics that Goneril and her sister Regan are exactly alike; "alike as two crabs," says the keenest critic of the guild. But nature never turns out two figures from the same model, and Shakespeare is nature. Regan has the tongue of a shrew; moreover, she appears only too ready in carrying out the suggestions of her older sister. But in judging her it must be remembered that both women acted with reference to their father under the greatest provocation.[1] If all the circumstances are studied carefully and without prejudice, it will be found that Regan, while indeed a woman of cold, selfish, and vindictive nature, stands no lower in the moral scale than hundreds of respectable people; and a number of indications strewn through the text make it appear that at her worst she is rather driven to evil deeds by awe of her strong-minded sister than drawn by the spontaneous promptings of an actively cruel nature. At all events, it is from Goneril that suggestions of novelties in cruelty invariably come. She it is that first disquantities her father's train. She it is that forestalls any attempt to recall the old king, as he rushes out into the darkness, by her cold-blooded sentence:

Lear II. iv. 293.

"'T is his own blame; hath put himself from rest,
And must needs taste his folly."

Under Lear's curses his second daughter winces; but Goneril merely laughs in derision at his terrible maledictions as the drivelling of a dotard.

But the difference between the sisters goes much deeper. Regan is free from treachery even to the point of unsuspiciousness; it is not her part to press the poisoned cup to the lips of one by whose death she will profit. But Goneril, aspiring to the

[1] See Barrett Wendell, William Shakespeare, p. 296 ff.

throne of an undivided England in company with Edmund, is capable of destroying every life that stands between her and her goal. Her sister we behold stricken by her potation ; her husband was to fall a victim to the same fate ; her brother-in-law must have been within the scope of her murderous plans, if we may judge from the way in which the news of his death is received ; it was her writ, as well as Edmund's, that was upon the life of Lear and of Cordelia. Nor was this, as we may infer, the first attempt she had made to kill her father. Before even the slight excuse that he had harbored with her enemies was offered her, she had sought to disencumber herself of him. We learn from Gloucester that at the time Lear sought refuge with Regan there was "a plot of death upon him." III. vi. 96. We cannot with justice suspect the second sister, for she seems to be speaking in good faith when she says she will take care of her father gladly, provided he will dismiss his retinue. On the other hand, circumstantial evidence, which the careful reader will not fail to notice, points directly to Goneril as the guilty party. It is even possible that she had formed her resolution upon the very day on which the old king announced his purpose to lay down his authority. For her first words to Regan, after the partition of the kingdom, are dark hints about important plans concerning Lear, plans not to be thought about, but to be acted upon and "i' the heat."

But, after all, the exact time at which Goneril

became, in intention, a parricide is of minor consequence. She is in any event a monster, whereas Regan is no more than a heartless and undutiful woman. It is the older sister, therefore, that stands as the incarnation of brazen-faced iniquity in its most aggressive and shameless form.

What, then, will this ruthless creature do when her husband loads her with reproaches for her inhumanity and want of natural affection? Will she awake to a sense of the enormity of her offences? Will she melt with contrition? It might have been if within her breast there had dwelt some rudiments of a better nature. On the eve of the commission of a great crime many a perverted will finds resolution stayed by the presence of an enemy within the gates. But of Goneril's kingdom no such insurrection is recorded; for the historian, looking into her soul, found there no rebel armed against the governing power. Hence, when she is confronted with the awful picture of her inner life, she feels no sorrow, no remorse, because she lacks the preconditions. The rather, by that instinct of self-preservation which dwells alike in our best and worst impulses, rage and contempt arise. Reproach is met by recrimination, and Albany is scored as a milksop, a coward, a moralizing fool. Later, in the very moment when her sister is dying with poison that she has administered, and her plot to kill her husband lies open to the light of day, she still breathes defiance as in the time of her strength;

IV. ii. 50-59. Cf. Pericles IV. iii.

and with the words on her lips, "The laws are mine, not thine: who can arraign me for 't?" this unbending spirit goes forth to meet death. V. iii. 158.

Yet even in this woman there still slumbers a germ of the moral life. When Edmund, whom she loves, lies dying before her, she suspects double dealing, and at once raises the cry of treachery, the cry, that is, of wrong, not merely of injury. Inasmuch as her own sister is at that moment dying of the poison which she had herself mixed, such a complaint may seem the very acme of absurdity. That it is in the highest degree inconsistent is evident; hardly less so that it is supremely human. The principle is illustrated over and over again in the historical plays, and while every one is familiar with its less exaggerated manifestations, experience will show that there are no limits to its application. Goneril, then, possesses just sufficient conscience to be roused to moral indignation for a passing instant, when she believes a cruel injury has been done her and the man she loves, although she has not enough to feel the lightest touches of self-condemnation for the crimes by which she herself is to profit. V. iii. 151.

It is to Iago, then, that we must turn for Shakespeare's sole representative, in his later period, of the absolutely conscienceless being. With the moral vocabulary Iago is, indeed, well acquainted. By observation he has learned what others admire and hate. Hence, he can use terms expressive of praise and blame with perfect propriety. Such actions as his, he knows, people call the blackest sins; himself they would call a devil. We may accordingly overhear him saying, with admirable perspicuity:

> "When devils will the blackest sins put on,
> They do suggest at first with heavenly shows,
> As I do now."

Othello II. iii. 357.

But let no one be deceived by these linguistic attainments.

Students of criminal psychology have noticed that most criminals employ euphemistic terms in speaking of their misdeeds. In the language of the German vagabond, thieving is business (*Geschäft*). The French burglar and murderer, Lacenaire, used the same word in seeking to obtain an accomplice in his friend Avril: "We ought to go into business together," he urged — "nous devons mêler ensemble notre industrie."[1] In the thieves' jargon of England, according to the boy in Henry V., stealing was "purchase." From Pistol we learn it was also styled "convey." This characteristic of human nature — for it is not confined to those who come into conflict with the police — has sometimes occasioned much amusement among the thoughtless. But, as a matter of fact, the man who

Henry V. III. ii. 44.

Merry Wives I. iii. 32.

[1] Despine, Psychologie naturelle, Vol. II., p. 433.

in the very act of committing a crime can look upon his deed with unaverted eyes, has reached the last stage of moral insensibility. For him who palters with himself there is always some hope; for the clear-seeing criminal, never. Accordingly, when an immoral man applies to his own conduct the adjectives by which the race express their admirations and loathings, he demonstrates either complete atrophy of conscience, or a weak will, which knows and approves the better, and struggles, though in vain, against overmastering temptations.

It is to the former class that Iago belongs. Like Richard III., he can face the truth because insensible of its meaning. What feats of objectivity were possible to him is shown by a significant passage at the beginning of the fifth act. Having decided that Cassio must die — a point apparently not included in the original draft of his plan — he is reviewing after his characteristic fashion the grounds for his decision. Among them he finds this:

3 Henry VI. III. ii. 182. Richard III. I. i. 30, 37.

"[Cassio] hath a daily beauty in his life
That makes me ugly."

Othello V. i. 19.

Iago has discovered that people admire Cassio more than him, notwithstanding his "honesty" and desire to be useful. Such a state of affairs may be prejudicial to his interests. Indeed it had already proved so, for it had doubtless helped to bring about the promotion of the "bookish theoric" to the position he himself coveted. And certainly it had led to the selection of the same theorist in preference to the practical ancient as Othello's confidant in his love affairs. For this reason, then, Cassio must be thrust out of the way. But instead of saying to himself, as a better man would have done: Cassio must be killed, because people admire him more than me, he states his grounds with almost incredible coolness in purely objective terms: Cassio's character is more admirable than mine. Such an utterance would have been practically impossible had not these words been to him as are the names of colors to one born blind, who has mastered the science of optics.

Some critics have found it possible, however, to endow Iago with the rudiments of a conscience, because of a peculiarity in the accounts he gives himself of his own motives. As is well known, the utterances of the monologues in which these revelations appear are confused and at times contradictory. The facts themselves, nevertheless, seem perfectly clear. He desires Roderigo's money, Cassio's place; possibly, too, the satisfaction of avenging himself upon Othello for preferring a book-crammed student to a man of affairs like himself, and for being the (innocent) occasion of false reports about his wife's infidelity. Though with regard to this matter of revenge, we may be sure that it would never have been allowed to interfere with what he considered his profit; while the fact that at the end he tries to drag Othello into the same net with himself can be explained by other motives than malevolence.[1] Most of all he lusts for a sense of his own power, and like Nietzsche, he knows nothing of the strength that dedicates itself to bearing the burdens of others. He therefore finds an actual enjoyment in his villainy, not primarily because he wants revenge, as is the conventional opinion, but because he delights in the sense of strength and skill that is awakened by successful intrigue.[2] He chuckles over his disguise and plays with it; he becomes so fascinated with the game that he half forgets the ends for which it was originally undertaken, and we hear about his marital jealousy of the Moor gnawing his inwards, and even of a similar jealousy of Cassio.

Cf. II. iii. 342, ff.

II. i. 304–316.

The palpable absurdity of his believing such suspicions, and of their "gnawing his inwards," even if he did believe them, is so great that many critics, following Coleridge, have discovered in these utterances the workings of conscience seeking some justification for the deeds it beholds committed. There is, however, no necessity for such an assumption. A cold-blooded calculating-machine like Iago must always have some ulterior end in view in everything he does. Are there not many excellent people who can never take a walk or go upon a journey without inventing some

1 See below, p. 126.

2 See Hazlitt, Characters of Shakespeare's Plays: Othello.

8

errand or call of business by way of a pretext? Iago is one of this class. Starting out to get money, position, and a taste of revenge *en route*, he is so far carried away by his delight in the hunt that to keep his self-respect as a rational being he has to invent as many reasons as his imagination can rake together to justify himself in taking the enormous risks he is incurring. Calculation, not conscience, is the only explanation needed for his "motive hunting." Calculation and a passion for intrigue explain the overwhelming majority of his words and deeds. The little that remains outside springs from sources not a whit more pure.

How Iago will act when his trap finally closes upon himself is foreshadowed in the analysis just made. Devoid as he is of all moral sensibility, he betrays neither sorrow nor shame as the network of his villainy is at length unravelled in the sight of the world, and his victims lie stricken before his eyes. He confesses just enough to secure a
V. ii. 296–7. companion in punishment, then closes his lips forever. Unrelenting, cold as the remorseless ice of an Alpine glacier, he is led away in silence to the torture chamber.

Does Iago live in this real world of ours? Can a human mother bring forth such a monster? The answer of transcendentalism is unequivocal. In the most emphatic terms Kant affirms and reaffirms the doctrine that "there is no man so depraved that in transgressing [the moral law] he would not feel a resistance, and an abhorrence of himself, so that he must put a force on himself."[1] The very existence of transcendentalism is bound up with the maintenance of this position. For the categorical ought is the offspring of pure reason, and pure reason, as the source of the fundamental principles of all forms of knowledge, is an essential element of even the most primitive human mind. Moreover, the purpose of the creation of man lies in his reducing the inner world of impulse and the outer world of blind force to a cosmos governed by reason's law. Obviously nature cannot be represented as defeating its own ends by creating instruments that lack the fundamental requisite for the performance of their appointed function.

Whom, then, shall we believe, Kant or Shakespeare? As was promised in the introduction to this study, the question of the objective value of Shakespeare's delineations has hitherto been kept in the background. At this point, however, an exception to the previously observed policy seems to be called for. In the first place, as the outcome of carefully conducted researches carried on by a large number of investigators during the past forty years, there has come into existence a group of important principles that are accepted by all authorities regardless of what other ethical and metaphysical theories they may happen to hold. Here, for once, then, we can test Shakespeare's

[1] Kant, Metaphysik der Sitten; Einleitung zur Tugendlehre. Abbott's Translation, p. 290, note.

fidelity to nature by criteria more objective than individual prejudices and fancies. In the second place, as we have already seen, and as we shall have farther opportunity to discover in our study of Macbeth, Shakespeare's criminals are constantly being misinterpreted through ignorance of the character of their prototypes in our own world. A brief review of certain of the results of criminal psychology may accordingly prove of genuine service to the cause of Shakespearean criticism.

The most important and startling of these results is one that vindicates in every detail Shakespeare's portrait of Iago. As all students of moral pathology are agreed, there exists a type of man to which the name born or instinctive criminal has been given.[1] The essential characteristics of this class are two in number: first, complete moral insensibility, revealed by absence of all repugnance to the suggestion of crime before the deed and of remorse after the commission. This, of course, does not mean that the criminal is unaware that the adjective "wrong" is by many people attached to certain classes of action, or that society or God dislikes such actions, and will strike back in revenge when the chance offers. What he lacks is the experiences that give the moral vocabulary its meaning to the good man. This phenomenon is often called moral imbecility. The second characteristic of the born criminal is a high degree of

[1] Both terms are misleading; the adjective "incorrigible" seems to me more satisfactory.

perversity, that is, the dominance of desires that are either directly anti-social, — as malicious cruelty and revengefulness,—or at least seducive, by which is meant peculiarly liable to grow at the expense of the higher interests. Most prominent among the latter are laziness, love of money, and lust.

The existence of this variety of *Homo sapiens* is in no way dependent upon the truth of theories about the shape of criminals' skulls, the development of their lower jaw, and much else of the same sort. For the existence of the psychological differentiæ of the class is not called in question by any opponent of the Italian school of criminal anthropology who has made a first-hand study of the subject, in whatever way he may be inclined to explain the facts.

Whether the term moral imbecility shall be restricted to those in whom conscience is absolutely a zero is, of course, a mere matter of terminology. Such persons are few in number, and the degrees of approximation to that state are innumerable. The ordinary basis of classification seems to be obtained by including under the name born criminal those who have exhibited entire absence of moral sensibility with regard to such capital or penitentiary offences as they may be known to have committed.

The evidence for the existence of moral imbecility is varied in nature and only too abundant in amount. We may lay it down as a universal law that remorseful guilt will confess when confronted with the proof of its evil deeds. In fact, there are many cases on record where the unsuspected but repentant criminal has voluntarily surrendered himself into the hands of the law. In not a few of these instances the motive has been a craving for punishment, born of moral indignation against the lower nature to which surrender has been made.[1] But the born criminal never confesses until the evidence against him is absolutely overwhelming, and often not even then. Furthermore, he disclaims all feelings of sorrow and repentance; he openly gloats over past success, or mourns over failure; he often slanders the injured party from the dock out of pure malice, under circumstances where he cannot suppose he will thereby change the outcome of the trial; and finally, he is given to abusing the police, the jury, or the judge, after his conviction. Occasionally he displays some feeling at his trial, but it is very remote in nature from remorse. Despine relates that a murderer twenty-two years of age on being brought to trial manifested no concern of any kind till informed that in the room of his victim, where he and his accomplice had succeeded in finding only eighty francs, a purse of fifteen hundred francs was concealed. Thereupon he burst into tears, exclaiming, "Oh, I told Chopin that it did n't

[1] This seemingly paradoxical emotion is exhibited in more than one of Shakespeare's characters: *e. g.*, Posthumus in Cymbeline. See V., iv., 3–29; v., 210–225.

pay to kill a man for eighty francs."[1] Moreover, when the wife murderer sleeps quietly for two or three nights in the bed by the side of the victim of his knife, and when the parricide is found in a saloon on the evening of the murder smoking calmly and watching with interest a game of billiards, then we are entitled to infer that remorse can hardly be disturbing their peace of mind. More striking than any other class of evidence is that exhibiting the attitude of many criminals towards God. Take as an example the following typical case. "A wife who was poisoning her husband wrote to her accomplice: 'He is not well. . . Oh, if God would have pity on us, how I would bless Him! When he complains [of the effects of the poison] I thank God in my heart.' And he answers, 'I will pray to Heaven to aid us.' And she again, 'He was ill yesterday. I thought that God was beginning His work. I have wept so much that it is not possible God should not have pity on my tears.'"[2] In their expectation of the approbation and sympathy of an all-seeing and impartial spectator, these murderers show beyond the possibility of mistake how far they are removed from self-condemnation and shame.

The impression that the layman carries away from the reading of such reports is confirmed by the concurrent testimony of those who have had

[1] Psychologie naturelle, Vol. II., p. 416.

[2] Havelock Ellis, The Criminal, p. 158.

the best opportunities for studying the criminal at first hand. The brilliant Russian author, Dostoieffsky, who spent several years in a Siberian prison, declares that he never met with one instance of moral suffering caused by the memory of a crime. "I have," he continues, "frequently heard convicts relate the most terrible crimes, the most unnatural deeds, laughing heartily at the recollection of them."[1] Perhaps the most exhaustive investigation ever made into this subject is that undertaken by the eminent Italian authority, Ferri, in preparation for his work on homicide. Of seven hundred criminals, murderers and thieves, whom he examined, more than ten per cent, he tells us, gave "absolute proof by the shamelessness of their behavior of the entire absence of remorse;" and the probable proportion of the completely indifferent and unrepentant is placed at thirty-five per cent.[2]

Troubled by some vague suspicion of such facts, transcendentalism has at times shifted its position. Moral insensibility is admitted, but is asserted to be the result of a long-continued course of wrong-doing. Thus it is said that "a man to be what Iago is, when we see him, must have gone through much perversion and many gradations of evil."[3] This does not seem to be Shakespeare's view. Iago

[1] Dostoieffsky, Buried Alive, chap. i.

[2] Lombroso, The Criminal (*L'uomo delinquente*), German Translation, Vol. I., pp. 348–350.

[3] Giles, Human Life in Shakespeare, p. 116.

is but twenty-eight; while of Richard III. his own mother bears the impressive testimony:

"Tetchy and wayward was thy infancy;
Thy school-days frightful, desperate, wild, and furious,
Thy prime of manhood daring, bold, and venturous."

Richard III. IV. iv. 168.

Again the dramatist and the criminal psychologist are at one. Despine's classical work contains examples of moral imbecility from every period of life, beginning with twelve years. One of Feuerbach's worst cases is a youth of fourteen.[1] Moral imbecility may thus be due to a congenital taint.

We must accordingly face the fact that there are human beings in whom not the slightest trace of moral sensibility has ever been discovered. However, among the morally imbecile, as this term was defined on page 117, there sometimes appear faint traces of a better nature. Goneril's dark heart we have seen lighted for an instant by a gleam of moral indignation. Macbeth and Lady Macbeth were true to each other. The importance of understanding these two tragic figures, the most subtle delineations in the long line of Shakespeare's criminals, will justify us in dwelling for a moment upon these inconsistencies of the human will.

Absence of remorse means *inter alia* complete indifference to the sufferings of the victim. But

[1] Feuerbach, Aktenmässige Darstellung merkwürdiger Verbrechen, chap. xxviii.

with this leaden apathy may go some considerable capacity for sharing the joy and sorrow of one or two intimate associates. Certain poisoners and other murderers have even been notably charitable; although those who ought to know assert that such benevolence is mixed with much alien material. Again, there are cases on record where no affection, not even the slightest, has shown itself for any human being. On the other hand, the emotion need not be wholly wanting, and it occasionally occurs in great intensity. For example, Lombroso declares that one of the most ferocious female criminals he ever knew was passionately fond of children.

It must be added, however, that what affection and sympathy these miserable beings possess is apt to be wholly capricious in its workings. Lacenaire, a brutal thief and murderer, of whom we shall hear again, declared that he was never overcome by the sight of his victim's corpse: "When I kill a person I have no more feeling about it than when I drink a glass of wine," are his own words. But he admitted that he was overcome with sorrow at the death of his cat. To save its life he risked his own on the very day that he murdered an old lady and her son for their money.[1] Perhaps the most extraordinary instance of one-sided sympathy ever chronicled is that told by Lombroso on the authority of Paul Lindau: "A man by the name of Schunicht murdered one of his former mistresses

[1] Lombroso, *opus cit.*, Vol. I., pp. 301, 317.

in the most brutal manner and with an indifference absolutely revolting. He had already left the house, when it occurred to him that the body might remain undiscovered for weeks, and in that event the canary belonging to the murdered woman would starve to death. Thereupon Schunicht retraced his steps, scattered enough food upon the floor of the cage to last the bird for several days, and opened the cage-door and the window in the adjoining room so that in any event the bird could make its escape."[1]

This anomalous trait is sometimes accompanied by another characteristic even more paradoxical. Given the rudiments of sympathy, it will sometimes assume the form of sentimentality. By this is meant playing the rôle of the sympathetic and generous mind, not merely before the world, but also before oneself, the actor evidently deceiving himself more or less for the time, and enjoying the resulting emotion; just as some people who never give way to resentment in any form delight in imagining that they have savage tempers, and others like to think of themselves as unhappy for the sake of the pleasures of self-pity thereby gained. Says that profound student of criminal humanity, Anselm von Feuerbach: "There is an intimate relation, especially in cold natures, between the cravings of romantic emotionalism and the sentimentality that, driven by a kind of necessity, titillates the inner sense by what is not really felt, but merely imagines itself felt; that attempts to palm off upon itself

[1] Lombroso, *opus cit.*, Vol. I., p. 318.

and the world mere grimaces in the place of genuine passions, thereby poisoning forever the source of the fundamental certitudes, the emotional life. . . . The genuine feelings are soon smothered by the spurious, which explains the fact that sentimentality is compatible with the most complete hardness of heart and even with active cruelty."[1]

A sufficient illustration of this principle is afforded by the "literary remains" with which certain of these choice spirits have enriched the world. No more malignant fiend was ever cursed with life than Thomas Wainewright, the poisoner. "Yet the chief characteristic of his essays," says Ellis, "is their sentimentality. Himself he describes as the possessor of a soul whose nutriment is love, and its offspring, art, music, divine song, and still holier philosophy."[2] Reading such flowing lines, we shall not be surprised to learn that when the muses smile upon him, the moral imbecile may become the poet of love and friendship. A typical example presents itself in the notorious Lacenaire.

Lacenaire has perhaps been sufficiently characterized in what was said of him above. Yet there may be profit in having a more concrete idea of this strange personality as the representative of a class, and I therefore quote briefly from his biography as given by Despine.[3] On trial for his life

[1] Feuerbach, *opus cit.*, p. 15.

[2] Havelock Ellis, *opus cit.*, p. 153. His biography is given in brief by Ellis, p. 12 ff., and p. 127. On this subject cf. Feuerbach, *opus cit.*, p. 358.

[3] *Opus cit.*, Vol. II., p. 423 ff.

on thirty different counts, — burglaries, forgeries, assaults, and murders, — his interest seemed to be completely centered in presenting a good appearance to the world contained within the court-room walls. "He seated himself upon the prisoner's bench with complete self-possession, and talked to his lawyer with a smile upon his lips. He acted as if he had no part whatever in the trial that was about to begin, an attitude which he maintained throughout, and which appeared to the spectators as posing." This was no comedy intended to deceive the court, for, the evidence against him being absolutely complete, he admitted his guilt from the first. He listened without emotion to the reading of the long list of his crimes, and later described them in an indifferent and flippant tone which filled his hearers with horror. At times he smiled agreeably, at other times laughed heartily, as in giving an account of the murder of a girl who possessed information that might compromise him with the police. He lured her into his room, induced her to drink a bottle of wine with him, and thereupon stabbed her. This adventure, as he related it, he seemed to find very amusing.

The following incident in his trial will throw additional light upon his character. A double murder had been committed some time before, but no clue to the perpetrators had been found. Lacenaire, since he had nothing to lose, announced himself as the murderer, and affably informed the authorities that he had two accomplices whose names he gave, and whose whereabouts he disclosed. His motive in thus ruining his comrades was not revenge for some real or fancied wrong. It was merely the desire for company that misery feels, a phenomenon described clearly in the following report of another trial taken from the same rich storehouse: "I was perfectly willing to kill, I did n't mind it a bit, for they had promised to pay me for it; but I wanted Joseph to strike the blow with me, so that if I was caught I should not get into trouble alone." [1] Lacenaire had his reward. His accomplices were executed with him. When one of these unfortunate beings, who persisted in denying his guilt, fell into a paroxysm of fury at the completeness of the evidence against him, Lacenaire laughed till the tears rolled down his cheeks.

Such was the man who, under sentence of death, his execution but a few weeks distant, unrepentant and devoid of shame, was capable of writing a poem beginning with the following lines.[2]

"Maudissez-moi, j'ai ri de vos bassesses,
J'ai ri des Dieux, pour vous seuls inventés;
Maudissez-moi: mon âme, sans faiblesses,
Fut ferme et franche en ses atrocités.
Pourtant cette âme était loin d'être noire,
Je fus parfois béni des malheureux . . .
A la vertu si mon coeur eût pu croire,
N'en doutez pas, j'eusse été vertueux."

[1] Despine, Vol. II., p. 175. Cf. above, p. 113.
[2] Lombroso, *opus cit.*, Vol. I., p. 424.

In a few born criminals, I repeat, what little sympathy they possess takes the form of sentimentality.

Weakness of sympathy is accompanied usually, though not invariably, by imperfect development of autopathy, or interest in one's own future. Where the imagination is too sluggish to enable its possessor to put himself into another man's place, it is likely to fail when he attempts to project himself into scenes and conditions not immediately connected with the imperious present. Thus, like the savage and the infant, he may be absolutely indifferent to even the foreseen evils of to-morrow. Then it happens that he will commit crimes in order to get money for a few days' debauchery, although, as he afterwards admits, he was perfectly aware all the time that detection and punishment, this often involving the death penalty, would be the inevitable consequence.

> "Bien fou, ma foi, qui sacrifie
> Le présent au temps à venir,"

these lines of Lacenaire appear to represent the maxim upon which he habitually acts.[1] The following incident described by Dostoieffsky shows how it works in practice. Dontoff "was brought before the court martial, and sentenced to run the gauntlet. He was . . . mortally afraid of physical pain. He managed to secrete a knife about his person, and on the eve of the fatal day, he at-

[1] They follow immediately his above-quoted lamentation for the virtues he never possessed.

tempted to stab one of his officers, as he entered the cell. He was perfectly aware that by this act he only aggravated his punishment, and yet he did it merely for the sake of having the terrible moment put off for a few days, at the utmost."[1]

Among other ways the sovereignty of the present shows itself in indifference to punishment in a future life. Comparatively few criminals are atheists, and few deny the existence of a life beyond the grave, where man must render an account of the deeds done in the body. Sometimes their indifference about consequences is really due to moral obtuseness; they cannot see that they have done anything to awaken the wrath of God. Others with more intelligence admit the fact but do not care.

This principle of criminal psychology is illustrated by Shakespeare over and over again. "For the life to come, I sleep out the thought of it," says Autolycus. Not different was the attitude of his more famous predecessor. In his tilts with Prince Hal, Falstaff can treat eternal damnation as a huge joke. In a different mood, when admonished in straightforward English of the need to repent, he thrusts the suggestion from him; there is a momentary pang of terror and the incident is ended. But when death comes to his bedside and says, "To-day," the old, lifelong indifference vanishes like

Winter's Tale IV. iii. 30.

1 Henry IV. I. ii. 102–9.

2 Henry IV. II. iv. 250–5.

[1] *Opus cit.*, chap. iv.

a dream, and he who once spared neither heaven nor hell in his jests may now be heard calling in agony upon God to avert the doom that he had never doubted would one day be his. It was not otherwise with Richard III.; it was not otherwise with Macbeth. The Thane of Cawdor, in the full flood of his ambition, looking the certainty of unending torment fairly in the face, declares that if he could only be assured of success in this life he would not hesitate to "jump the life to come." The denunciation of eternal punishment, frequently proclaimed to be a specific against deliberate surrender to criminal suggestion, proves itself powerless in just those persons for whom it is most needed.

Henry V. II. iii. 9–41.

Macbeth I. vii. 7.

There is much else in Shakespeare's portrayal of criminals that it would be of advantage to study, if it were not that anything like a complete treatment of the subject would take us too far from the main course of our inquiry. His knowledge is by no means confined to the moral imbecile. All the classes into which modern authorities have divided the variety "criminal" he knew and described, adjusting the kind and degree of their emotional reaction to the accomplished deed with a nicety and a precision that other men could have attained only after years devoted to the subject. Again, the principle laid down by Lombroso and Ferrero: "In general the moral physiognomy of the born female criminal approximates strongly to that of the male,"[1]

[1] The Female Offender, p. 187.

he observed and illustrated in Macbeth, King Lear, Pericles (Dionyza), and Cymbeline. Even the little things did not escape his notice. His thieves spend as quickly as they win. His vagabonds answer to the description of Locatelli: "Of all criminals they are the most jolly, so that they are gladly welcomed into whatever society they find themselves thrust."[1] Indeed we may assert without exaggeration that there is no one principle of criminal psychology that is at once important and *assured*, no proposition that would command the assent of all careful students who know the criminal at first hand, that cannot be derived from the Shakespearean drama.

1 Henry IV. I. ii. 37–43.

[1] Quoted by Lombroso, *opus cit.*, Vol. I., p. 378.

CHAPTER VI

THE FREEDOM OF THE WILL

As Shakespeare contemplated such characters as Richard and Iago, the profoundest problems of life must have come thronging in upon his mind. Is a man born to crime, because insensible to goodness, responsible for what he does? Can he properly be blamed for acting out his own nature? Again, what of the inner life of these creatures? They wreck others without a qualm: is it well with them? Finally, when they look upon the good man with contempt, as they do, is there any basis in the nature of things for their attitude? Or on what they themselves would admit to be facts, can they be shown to be mistaken?

As the outcome of his studies, Despine lays down the corollary that the moral imbecile is a completely irresponsible being. Devoid of all motive for seeking the good, he has no freedom to choose between the better and the worse, and without freedom there can be no responsibility. If this last statement were brought forward by moralists as a principle deduced by themselves from the data gathered during their investigations, it would have to be ignored in a study that aims merely to present the phenomenology of the moral consciousness. But the believer in free-will does not and cannot separate his own convictions on this subject from the opinions of the race. All men, he asserts, and must assert, from the savage to the sage, regard freedom as an essential condition of responsibility; and accordingly where they impute the latter they postulate the former. An assertion of this nature properly belongs within the scope of our inquiry. Our examination into its validity will call for an answer to two questions: Does the common man regard himself and his neighbor as free? Does he limit responsibility by freedom?

Before entering upon a study of the subject, it is necessary to point out the ambiguity of the word freedom. It would be an easy matter to make out a list of ten or twelve senses in which it is used in standard ethical treatises. Fortunately for the reader, many of them may be neglected, but it will be impossible to take a single step without distinguishing at least four possible meanings of the term.

In the first place, then, the will, or, better, the person, may be said to be free in so far as he is able to do what he desires to do, and to refrain from doing what he desires not to do. This freedom may be limited by the forces of external nature, or the superior physical strength of other living beings. It may also be limited by agencies that are represented, more or less completely, in our own consciousness: the sneeze, the laugh, or the hysteria, which, let us try our utmost, prove to be uncontrollable; the impulses of suicidal and homicidal mania, and the like, that sweep a man away to actions which never for an instant have his consent, and which he views as he performs them with grief and horror.

In a second sense we may be said to be free when we are able to bring all our actions into conformity with our permanent desires. The sovereignty of the passing instant is broken. We act and in acting know we shall not be called upon to regret, except as new insight may show our deed to be something other than we had thought it. For better or worse our destiny is what in our coolest hours we would have it, in so far as destiny is determined by character.

Again, man is endowed with a third kind of freedom in so far as he is capable of becoming what he desires to be, *i. e.*, in so far as he has the power to modify and transform the character with which he was endowed at birth. This he can do through his control over his actions and thoughts, in virtue of the principle that impulses to action, if inoperative through a considerable portion of time, tend to lose their strength and in many cases actually disappear. In this way the clamorous passion, the untamed appetite, cowardice, inertia, and selfishness, may be gradually eliminated, and higher elements substituted in their place. The man whose early life was a chaos of conflicting impulses may thus attain ultimately to the peace that shall never be broken by rebellion. "'T is in ourselves that we are thus or thus. Our bodies are our gardens, to the which our wills are gardeners; so that if we will plant nettles, or sow lettuce, set hyssop and weed up thyme, supply it with one gender of herbs, or distract it with many, either to have it sterile with idleness, or manured with industry, why, the power and corrigible authority of this lies in our wills." The condition upon which this form of freedom rests is the will to use it. "Look, what I will not, that I cannot do," says Angelo, with profound truth. Whoever is sufficiently desirous of growing thyme or lettuce to manure the soil with industry shall have his reward. For others there can be only weeds.

Iago in Othello I. iii. 322.

M. for M. II. ii. 51.

The denial of freedom in any of these forms is the dogma of fatalism in the proper significance of that much-abused term. Fatalism as we find it in the popular thought of the ancient Greeks, and in Mohammedan theology, is primarily a doctrine of what happens to man, but it may be applied with equal propriety to what he does. It asserts that the will is not a factor in, but merely an impotent spectator of the struggle of life; that nothing comes to pass because we determine it shall be. Œdipus, for instance, is fated to kill his father and marry his mother. It would have made no difference how firmly he determined never to take a human life, and how tenaciously he held to his purpose.

He and his father must meet, if not in the narrow pass, then somewhere else; and if Œdipus had still remained firm, his will would have been stricken with paralysis and, as in an attack of homicidal mania the mother may plunge the knife into her child's heart in the very instant in which, with agonized cries, she urges him to flee, so Œdipus would have beheld his own hand striking the blow that he was powerless to stay. The will refuses its consent; but the deed is done in despite of the will.

It is obvious that for actions of this kind no man can be held responsible. For responsibility means that a man is the proper object of moral judgment because of his deed. Now, moral judgment is directed to character, and here is an action that is not the outcome of the character, and that sheds no light whatever upon the direction in which it is moving. All members of the European races recognize this fact to-day, and all hold that at least some actions are not fated. As no contemporary moralist would dispute this statement, there is no need of dwelling upon it at greater length.

But many philosophers assert the existence of a fourth kind of freedom, freedom from the law of causation. When a certain course of action is adopted or decided upon, they hold that this decision or determination has no cause. The idea of doing it suggested itself, of course, in accordance with the laws of association; the idea of the rejected alternative presented itself to the mind in the same way. But the act of acceptance or rejection is itself causeless; in vain would you seek in the man's character or past habits, interests or purposes, for the ground of its being. If it were possible for every condition, external and internal, to be repeated, there would be the same chance that the second time the acceptance would be replaced by rejection. This view is called indeterminism.

A large number of authorities maintain, on the other hand, that the law of causation holds without exception in the mental as in the physical world. In so far as they believe in the autonomy of the will, as asserted in the preceding paragraphs, they hold that a man's actions are the outcome of his character, as it is at the time. A person may gradually change his character, if he wishes to; he can conquer his passions, appetites, and bad habits, if he will. But the condition of his even attempting it is a wish to do so. And if the opposition is strong, no vague, weak longings will suffice; the change must be desired intensely. Now all the elements of his character, including his desire for improvement, must have had a beginning in time; he who "has them," as we say, did not create them, for they are the inmost parts of himself. They arise and grow according to laws that we did not make and cannot alter. The doctrine that maintains the unbroken continuity of the causal series is called determinism. We now see that it has two forms, which may be called fatalistic and autonomic. Our problem may accordingly be stated as follows:

What attitude does the common man take, whether virtually or explicitly, to the position of autonomic determinism?

It will be obvious that determinism must affirm and indeterminism deny the possibility of forecasting the actions of human beings. Not but that indeterminism may be compatible with a certain amount of prophecy. No man can act except upon suggestions that come to him, and the appearance of these suggestions in the arena of consciousness is admitted on all hands to be rigidly determined. Furthermore — and this has often been overlooked — indeterminists are entitled to hold that a man cannot act upon suggestions that do not appeal to him;[1] the freedom they contend for consists solely in an uncaused choice between alternatives that really attract. Thus an indeterminist does not stultify himself when he declares his friend to be incapable of a falsehood, provided he knows him well enough to feel justified in asserting that the opportunity to gain an end through lying would never arouse in his friend even the slightest inclination to take advantage of it. Where contending desires dispute the field, however, there, if indeterminism is right, prevision becomes absolutely impossible. No one can tell, at any rate in matters of right and wrong, how such a preference will turn. Our problem accordingly takes this form: In cases of genuine moral con-

[1] So Despine. Cf. James, Principles of Psychology, II., 577, note.

flict, does the common man ever consider himself capable of forecasting the outcome?

The answers given by Shakespeare to this question are strikingly uniform and consistent throughout. They are formulated once for all in a speech of Warwick in Henry IV. The king has been recalling how the deposed Richard long ago foretold Northumberland's present treason. Warwick replies:

> "There is a history in all men's lives,
> Figuring the nature of the times deceased;
> The which observed, a man may prophesy,
> With a near aim, of the main chance of things
> As yet not come to life, which in their seeds
> And weak beginnings lie intreasured.
> Such things become the hatch and brood of time;
> And by the necessary form of this
> King Richard might create a perfect guess
> That great Northumberland, then false to him,
> Would of that seed grow to a greater falseness;
> Which should not find a ground to root upon,
> Unless on you.
>
> *King.* Are these things then necessities?
> Then let us meet them like necessities."

2 Henry IV. III. i. 80.

This passage contains a distinct declaration that conduct is the necessary outcome of character, and accordingly in so far as we know the character we can foretell the conduct. Since we can never gain a complete acquaintance with the inner life, we can, it is true, only prophesy "with a near aim." But no hint is given that our power of prevision is confined to hopeless iniquity and inflexible sainthood. Northumberland himself, while a weak and unprincipled man, does not appear to have been wholly bad. His acquaintances seemingly had no reason to doubt that better impulses were known to him; the question with them was, would they predominate? Richard and Warwick evidently thought not. And yet on the indeterministic theory there is no basis even for conjecture. The chances are one to one, and if the range of your calculation is sufficiently extensive that proportion will be realized. But any one person may have a run of luck, good or bad, as he may at *rouge-et-noir*, and therefore all prediction about individuals is impossible.

It may of course be objected that this statement of Warwick is a mere *obiter dictum*, or that at all events we have no more right to hold Shakespeare's other characters responsible for this expression of opinion than for good old Duncan's absurdity: "There's no art to find the mind's construction in the face." **Macbeth I. iv. 12.** The principle on which this objection is based is perfectly sound. Here, however, it avails nothing, for one of the most common phenomena in our dramas is the prediction of human action. Almost any of the histories or tragedies would supply satisfactory illustrative material.

In Othello, Act II., scene i., line 254, Roderigo declares to Iago, "I cannot believe that in her [Desdemona]; she's full of most blessed condition." This certainly looks like the spirit of prophecy; but we shall do well not to treat it as evidence of the deterministic attitude, for it may mean: Desdemona is absolutely incapable of temptation in this direction. But when Lodovico, witnessing the last wild outbreak of Othello's rage, asks in sur-
Othello IV. prise: "Is this the nature whom passion
i. 276. could not shake?" but one inference from his words seems possible. For the very point of the question lies in the implication that Othello is not a passionless nature, not one whom passion never tried to shake, but rather one against whose granite will its waves had hitherto dashed in vain. Again we seem to have an unequivocal statement in Cassio's exclamation when Othello falls by the stroke of his own dagger,

"This did I fear, but thought he had no
V. ii. 359. weapon;
For he was great of heart."

Possibly it may be objected that Cassio means no more than that he had considered the chances in favor of suicide to be even, but I venture to assert such an interpretation would have surprised Cassio.

The tragic interest of Antony and Cleopatra centres in the downfall of a nature rich in possibilities for good. The Roman triumvir is no moral imbecile, nor is he one condemned by a hereditary curse to live only for the passing moment. Once he could bear deprivation and suffering in the pursuit of power and fame. "Antony, leave thy lascivious wassails," cries Octavius:

"When thou once
Wast beaten from Modena, where thou slew'st
Hirtius and Pansa, consuls, at thy heel
Did famine follow; whom thou fought'st against,
Though daintily brought up, with patience more
Than savages could suffer: thou didst drink
The stale of horses, and the gilded puddle
Which beasts would cough at: thy palate then did deign
The roughest berry on the rudest hedge;
. . . . . .
And all this . . .
Was borne so like a soldier, that thy cheek
So much as lank'd not."

A. and C. I. iv. 55.

The ambition which enabled Antony at that time to endure even to the uttermost never became to him an unsubstantial dream. Furthermore, he had a genius for friendship, the basis of continuous wedded love; witness the devotion he enkindled in his followers. He was generous even to his worst enemies, his disloyal friends. When his most trusted general, Enobarbus, forsook him for the winning side, he sent after the fugitive his chests and treasures, which the latter had been unable to take with him. He never ceased to realize his own degradation. We might suspect it from this little incident of Enobarbus' treasures, if other proof were wanting.

Act IV., scene v.

Once these forces almost dominated his life. There was a time when, had he been wedded to an Octavia, he might have ruled his share of the world, another Augustus. But in the toils of Cleopatra he becomes a different man. One who knew him as he once had been wonders to see him slight the most important business in order that "not a minute of [their] lives should stretch without some pleasure." No one seems to think of the chance theory; the only explanation which an old follower can suggest is that he is much changed. Enobarbus, having watched stage by stage the development of the new Antony, does not hesitate to predict the outcome of the marriage with Octavia. "He will to his Egyptian dish again: then shall the sighs of Octavia blow the fire up in Cæsar; and that which is the strength of their amity shall prove the immediate author of their variance." Enobarbus includes three complicated

I. i. 46.

II. vi. 134.

personalities, it will be observed, within the scope of his prophecy. Waiving all discussion as to the nature of his data with respect to the strong, single-minded triumvir and his noble sister, he certainly could not count in the case of Antony upon the total destruction of the desire to play a great part on the world's stage, of regard for the interests of his followers, of honor and self-respect. For still it remained true that now and then a "Roman thought" would strike him, pathetic witness of the impulses still stirring within his soul. But the shrewd old general believed he could foretell, when the two alternatives were presented to his master, which would be chosen.

The only phase of the problem of the determination of human conduct that Shakespeare's people ever discuss is the causes of character. Of the various theories that the ingenuity of man has put together the two that are most in favor are heredity and the influence of the stars. It is only on the latter hypothesis that Kent can explain the difference between Cordelia and her sisters. Gloucester goes farther; the heavenly bodies can actually change a character already formed. Edmund, the superior intellect of the play, denies this and indeed the entire theory of "spherical predominance." For this reason he has been supposed to be an indeterminist. Such an inference, however, ignores the existence of a large number of alternatives, any one of which he may have held; as the influence of education and surroundings, the miraculous interference of God or the devil, and much else. If Edmund believed that natural endowment is the most important factor in the making of character, by the side of which nurture is a comparatively insignificant though not entirely impotent force, natural endowment in turn being determined largely though not exclusively by heredity, he will be in agreement with what seems to have been the views of a large number of Shakespeare's people. Some of these in their surprise at the failure of heredity in a particular instance give the most unequivocal expression of belief in the potency of innate volitional capacities.[1]

On this subject I believe we for once get a glimpse of the dramatist's own opinions. It is an invariable rule with him that, however dark the course of a story, its final scene shall close with an outlook upon a better world. Thus in Romeo and Juliet the death of the lovers leads to a reconciliation between two great families. In Macbeth and King Lear the floods of misrule and civil war finally subside, leaving in possession of the throne rulers strong, honorable, and humane, who — on the deterministic theory — may be expected to inaugurate an era of good government. Even in Othello we have the satisfaction of knowing that Iago's career is ended; he can poison no more lives.

[1] Rich. III., I. iii. 229–231; Rich. II., V. iii. 60–63; All 's Well, I. ii. 19–22; Lear, IV. iii. 34–37; Timon, IV. iii. 271–4; Pericles, IV. iii. 23–25; Tempest, IV. i. 188–189.

This rule seems at first sight grossly violated in All's Well that Ends Well, and that in the very teeth of the promise conveyed in its title. The end which is to be so delightful is the reconciliation of Bertram with Helena after his flight from her upon their forced marriage. Now, Helena is one of the most perfect of Shakespeare's characters. She represents that combination of strength and devotion which, as we have seen, is repeatedly declared to be the complete embodiment of moral beauty. Though living as a dependant in a titled family she has the intelligence and courage to recognize herself as the equal of the young master of the house. To obtain his love she risks the displeasure of her foster-mother, death at the king's court, and, what means most to her, dishonor through misinterpretation of her motives. Constantly called upon to act in circumstances of great difficulty she exhibits a quickness of apprehension, tact, decision, and firmness, that alone would render her a marked character. Her purity of mind is never doubtful in the most delicate situations. Sincerity shines through every deed. It wins at the outset the spectator of the play, who knows from the moment of her appearance that this young girl is no adventuress. It wins the king. Even total strangers trust her. As her sincerity evokes confidence, her sweetness and beauty procure her the love of man and woman.

So much for Helena. "Look you now what follows." Bertram is indeed a man of courage, spirit, and ability, but that is the end. In matters that do not concern war he must be set down as a weak, gullible, and withal unprincipled cad. As Hamlet reveals his ideals through his friendship with Horatio, so we are entitled to infer the worst from the ascendency that Parolles gains over Bertram. In Hamlet, ideals never get worked out into life; it is the reverse with Bertram. His companions at court, won at a glance by the loveliness of Helena, are more than willing to marry the physician's daughter whom the king's gratitude has permitted to select a husband. He who knows her best alone refuses. When forced under the yoke by the fiat of the king which neither party may resist, he follows up blindness and pride by a display of insolence, and the insolence is rather that of a child than of a man. His intrigue with Diana after his flight from Paris into Italy is as discreditable as an intrigue can be. He seeks to gain his will by promises that he does not intend to keep. Then confronted with the demand that he redeem his pledge, he turns and twists to avoid Diana's charges, blackening her character first in one way then in another. A study of the details of this episode will only serve to deepen the unpleasant impression made by its outlines.

Such, then, are the two principal characters of the play, a strong, noble woman and a spoiled, unprincipled boy. These are the people whose union for life is expected to call forth the exclamation: Well done! No wonder most readers turn away in disgust. The plot seems to have descended to the plane of a summer novel where the only object is to get two people married. Some readers may indeed comfort themselves with the thought that Helena will reform her wayward husband. But that appears like a vain hope; for reformation, as a process of cultivation, must have something to work upon. Nor, looking at the case in the abstract, is the percentage of success in this line of activity great enough to inspire with a high degree of confidence—let us say a father with marriageable daughters.

Nevertheless, the play, I believe, is neither "disappointing," "perplexing," nor "profoundly immoral." All does end well. The difficulties in which the poet has involved himself are due to his faithfulness to the original sources of the plot; but he has found a solution, and one that is simplicity itself. He merely makes us acquainted with the characters of Bertram's father and mother.

The distinguishing traits of the Countess are penetration, unselfishness, and the capacity for proportioning affection to real merit. This last she possesses in an extraordinary degree; it frees her from all prejudices of aristocratic birth; it makes her love Helena as her own daughter; it drives her to cast off for a time her son when he exhibits a pride, an insensibility to virtue in the low born, and a hardness of heart that are alien to her own nature. Her philosophy of life makes the love of Helena for Bertram seem as normal as if the girl had been the daughter of one of her titled neighbors.

The Count is dead, but his portrait has been carefully preserved for us as it lived in the memory of the king.

"In his youth
He had the wit which I can well observe
To-day in our young lords; but they may jest
Till their own scorn return to them unnoted
Ere they can hide their levity in honour:
So like a courtier, contempt nor bitterness
Were in his pride, or sharpness; if they were,
His equal had awaked them, and his honour,
Clock to itself, knew the true minute when
Exception bid him speak, and at this time
His tongue obey'd his hand: who were below him
He used as creatures of another place
And bow'd his eminent top to their low ranks,
Making them proud, as his nobility
In their poor praise he humbled."[1]

All's Well that Ends Well I. ii. 31.

The happy issue of the plot is thus entrusted to the workings of the principle of heredity. A hint of this solution is conveyed in the words

[1] The text of line 44 follows a conjecture of Hudson.

with which the king greets Bertram on the latter's presentation to him.

> "Youth, thou bear'st thy father's face;
> Frank nature, rather curious than in haste,
> Hath well composed thee. Thy father's moral parts L. 19.
> Mayst thou inherit too!"

We may look forward with confidence to the fulfilment of this hope. The boy has developed slowly, and his growth in the past has been in part retarded by unfavorable influences from without. But now that the proper environment has been supplied, his true nature may be trusted to appear. For the existence within him of the potentialities of all goodness is guaranteed by the character of his ancestry.

In a more famous play Shakespeare has taken the greatest pains to record his conviction that no absolute break is possible between our present and our past. The instantaneous transformation of Prince Hal from the boon companion of roysterers and cut-purses to the wise, self-restrained, and just king, was regarded by the chroniclers of his time as the result of a miracle. But this view of the matter is excluded with the greatest care in the dramas that describe his life. Every salient trait in the character of the king is either exhibited or asserted as existing in the prince: affection, generosity, the am- 2 Hen. IV. IV. iv. 21 ff. II. ii. 42–54.

1 Hen. IV. V. v. 22–31. 1 Hen. IV. III. ii. 132–158. V. ii. 52–69. 1 Hen. IV. V. i. 83–100. 2 Hen. IV. IV. iv. 31–32. 2 Hen. IV. II. ii. 5 ff.

bition that selects the noblest models for emulation, regard for the life and welfare of others, and hatred of sham and hypocrisy. His very excesses are represented as in part the outcome of some of his best qualities: his contempt for the artificial distinctions that are consecrated by court tradition; his love of the vigorous London lower-class life; his enjoyment of wit-combats and a hearty laugh. Nor were his frolics ever allowed to degenerate into mischief. Only one of them is of a really doubtful character, and in that the money which he helps to steal, or rather permits to be stolen, in order to perpetrate a joke upon Jack Falstaff, is returned to its owner the next day.

Had this play been the creation of a slightly later period, such hints would have been judged sufficient. The mature Shakespeare is perfectly content to be misunderstood by those who cannot or will not supplement the detached and momentary pictures of his score of scenes by images of a continuous life of which the fragments upon the stage are but the barest suggestion. As it is, however, we are supplied with a clean-cut declaration of the doctrine of natural development in its application to the newly crowned king. And as if to give it the maximum of emphasis it is put into the mouths of two churchmen.

Ely. The strawberry grows underneath the nettle
And wholesome berries thrive and ripen best
Neighbour'd by fruit of baser quality:
And so the prince obscured his contemplation
Under the veil of wildness; which, no doubt,
Grew like the summer grass, fastest by night,
Unseen, yet crescive in his faculty.

Henry V. I. i. 60.

Canterbury. It must be so; for miracles are ceased;
And therefore we must needs admit the means
How things are perfected.

A simple application, this, of the principle that men do not gather grapes from thorns or figs from thistles. But it totally ignores the possibility of that inner creation of motive force out of nothing for which indeterminism stands.

It may be of interest to note further that the just quoted confession of faith denies in the most unqualified manner one of the fundamental tenets of the Elizabethan church, St. Augustine's doctrine of grace. The official creed of the church as formulated in the Articles of 1563 affirms: "The condition of man after the fall of Adam is such, that he cannot turn and prepare himself by his own natural strength and good works, to faith and calling upon God. Wherefore we have no power to do good works, pleasant and acceptable to God, without the grace of God by Christ preventing us, that we may have a good will, and working in us, when we have that good will." Again the churchmen speak for Shakespeare. As he explains the crimes of the moral imbecile without invoking the agency of the devil, so he describes the unfolding life of the noble soul in terms that leave as little room for miracle as for chance. Was he not in this respect as far in advance of the theologians of his age as in his conception of mental disease he was beyond the vast majority of its physicians?

To return from Shakespeare to Shakespeare's people: wherever we have an opportunity to make the test we find them manifesting a belief in the determination of volition by character. Usually they think of character as mainly the outcome of heredity; sometimes, however, they attribute it rather vaguely to the miraculous interposition of supersensible powers; occasionally, on the other hand, to the stars. With but two exceptions, which will be considered below, the notion of a causeless volition apparently never even enters their minds.

Does the world look upon the man whose conduct can be foretold as a morally irresponsible being? The answer to this, the second of our two questions, is as clear and unequivocal as the answer to the first. In its approbation and reprobation of actions it asks only, do they really proceed from the character? It takes for granted that the bad will is bad, the good will, good, however they came to be such; in other words, that questions of quality or worth do not turn on theories of origin. Consult, in verification, that richest mine of ethical information, King Lear. Nothing but a miracle could make the King of France believe Cordelia capable of a great wrong; her nobility of character is for that reason none the less genuine and admirable in his eyes. Cordelia, the Fool, and ultimately Albany, understand the nature of Goneril through and through, and the two former foretell her actions as with a prophet's vision. Yet this woman appears to them no less hateful and despicable on that ground. Kent seems to believe that the characters of the three sisters are the product of stellar influences; this does not modify his judgment of what they are. Indeed, reprobation or admiration may be concomitant with an explicit recognition of the deterministic position. Richard III., for instance, is declared by Queen Margaret to have been

> "Seal'd in [his] nativity
> The slave of nature and the son of hell."

Richard III. I. iii. 229.

It does not occur to Margaret that this makes him any less loathsome. He is what he is, a foul blot on creation. Had his crimes been from first to last the outcome of chance, he could have been no more base or vile. So Timon judges the notoriety-seeking, pseudo-cynic Apemantus.

"Thy father . . .
Timon IV. iii. 271. . . . in spite put stuff
To some she beggar and compounded thee
Poor rogue hereditary."

The rogue hereditary is none the less a rogue.

The average layman, then, finds nothing incompatible with moral approbation in the conception of conduct as the necessary outcome of character. But certain speculative intellects have discovered difficulties in the deterministic doctrine of responsibility, and have asserted in consequence that a caused volition has no moral value. This view finds expression in Shakespeare's plays on two different occasions. Hamlet, waiting in company with Horatio for his father's ghost, moralizes as follows upon the Danish reputation for drunkenness:

"So, oft it chances in particular men,
That for some vicious mole of nature in them,
As, in their birth — wherein they are not guilty,
Since nature cannot choose his origin —
Hamlet I. iv. 23. . . . .
That these men,
Carrying, I say, the stamp of one defect,
Being nature's livery, or fortune's star, —
Their virtues else — . . .
Shall in the general censure take corruption
From that particular fault."

Whether it is an accident that this opinion is put into the mouth of a university student I cannot say; but I have often wondered whether we may not suppose that Hamlet picked it up from his lectures in philosophy at Wittenberg. At all events, I can find no satisfactory evidence that he uses any such principle in his concrete judgments of men
and women. His old friends, Rosen- III. iv. 203.
crantz and Guildenstern, he declares he
will trust as he will adders fang'd. At the same time he justifies his own action in sending them to
certain death on the ground that they V. ii. 57.
richly deserved their fate. We can ex-
tract indeterminism from this combination of circumstances only by assuming that, through a long succession of free choices of evil, these two young men had completely seared their conscience, so that at last their conduct had become rigidly determined. The guilt now imputed to them might thus really attach to their past decisions. Whether this was the ground on which Hamlet condemned them so mercilessly, he unfortunately neglects to inform us.

It would not be fair, however, to emphasize too much the difference between the philosopher and the layman. Their brains are of the same clay. It will, therefore, not be wonderful if an echo of the philosopher's perplexities is heard now and then in the world where men of action live and work. Shakespeare's second and last apologist for the criminal by heredity would count himself a member of this latter class.

In Antony and Cleopatra, Act I., scene iv., Octavius and Lepidus are discovered discussing the failings of their fellow-triumvir, Antony. To the bitter complaints of Octavius, Lepidus answers:

> "His faults in him seem . . . hereditary,
> L. 12. Rather than purchased; what he cannot change,
> Than what he chooses."

The language is a little ambiguous, but the voice sounds like the voice of the indeterminist. Whether the dramatist is here seeking to throw contempt upon this mode of whitewashing weakness and vice I will not undertake to decide, but there is much to suggest it. No excuse could have been more inappropriate under the circumstances, since Octavius might easily rejoin: It was all one to him why Antony could not be depended upon to perform the duties belonging to his position; what he had to deal with was the fact, and on any theory of its cause he was confronted with a condition that must come to an end. These
See ll. 16-32. thoughts, indeed, can be read between the lines of Octavius' reply. He completely ignores Lepidus' apology, continues to blame Antony without raising the question whether his faults could be changed or not, and asserts his own unwillingness to bear the burdens rolled upon his shoulders by another's voluptuousness.

Evidently Lepidus does not understand the indeterministic theory well enough to recognize the limits within which, even in the eyes of its friends, its excuses are relevant. Or, perhaps shaken by fear that if Antony falls the heir of Julius Cæsar may elect to rule the world alone, he is merely talking at random. This latter hypothesis has antecedent probabilities in its favor. Drama and history alike bear witness to the justice of the verdict pronounced by Antony soon after the establishment of the triumvirate.

"This is a slight unmeritable man,
Meet to be sent on errands.

. . . .

A barren-spirited fellow; one that feeds J. C. IV. i. 12, 13, 36-39.
On abjects, orts and imitations,
Which, out of use and staled by other
men,
Begin his fashion."

Lepidus seems conscious of his weakness. And it may have been but a fulfilment of his forebodings, when, after he had served Octavius' purpose, he was thrown aside like a worn-out garment.

The clever controversialist, Mr. Arthur Balfour, some years ago informed the public that modern determinism is bound to look upon the popular belief in free will as an illusion produced by natural selection. If society is to be kept alive, he imagines the argument to run, men must attribute to each other moral responsibility and therefore freedom; if, then, the belief in the latter is an illusion, its existence can only be explained by the elimination of those communities amongst which it failed to appear. If we may trust Shakespeare, however, this hypothesis is wholly gratuitous. For the kind of free will about which Mr. Balfour is talking is separated by a great gulf from the freedom in which the typical man believes. The men of the Elizabethan era and the men of to-day agree in recognizing the existence of a freedom from external forces that permits the character, in its actions, to show what it really is. And where this power of self-expression exists they praise and blame, or in other words, impute responsibility. The vast majority of the human race have never dreamed of a freedom of another kind. When a Hamlet and a Lepidus fall into perplexities, it is because they confuse the necessity that links action to character and the necessity that wrenches action away from character, and forces into the world deeds which the will itself would never consent to send forth.

CHAPTER VII

VIRTUE AND HAPPINESS

After Cornwall had blinded Gloucester, a servant who had witnessed the deed exclaimed, "I 'll never care what wickedness I do, if this man come to good." These words are the expression of a deeply rooted postulate of the human mind. In any tolerable order, it is felt, evil-doing must be followed by misfortune. In committing a wrong, the agent seizes upon a good that can become his only at the expense of some more important interest of another or others. Is this the end of the matter? Or is the world so constructed that the infraction of the laws of social welfare inevitably involves an additional breach in individual well-being?

Lear III. vii. 99.

When the nobler natures fall, there waits for them a penalty in the form of remorse. Impressive, if brief, glimpses of its power in minds susceptible in any degree to the higher impulses are afforded by the stories of Queen Gertrude and Enobarbus. And when in the blindness of passion a high-strung, sensitive man strikes with a deadly blow the being he loves best, as in Cymbeline and The Winter's Tale, the law that we reap more than we sow is fulfilled to the letter.:

> "Though those that are betray'd
> Cymbeline III. iv. 87. Do feel the treason sharply, yet the traitor
> Stands in worse case of woe."

But at least in its application to remorse this principle is not of universal validity. It would hold for Imogen as it held for Posthumus; but Iago's hard heart could laugh its threatenings to scorn. Remorse is due to the awakening of moral sensibilities that have been temporarily drugged into torpor; therefore, it can never trouble those in whom conscience is either dead or unborn. The moral imbecile and the hardened criminal in all cases, and men of only average moral aptitudes in some cases, are thus proof against everything except extra-moral suffering. Do penalties of this class appear, then, where conscience is inert and remorse fails?

That the wicked man often brings trouble upon himself as the direct result of his wickedness, it requires no argument to prove. Such misfortune may take on a score of forms that are sufficiently well known, as disease, imprisonment, and failure. But evil-doing has indirect effects no less disastrous that are frequently overlooked. It has been said that the worst punishment of the liar is not that others cannot believe him, but that he cannot believe others. This principle, of course, holds for every variety of treachery. Its workings can be traced without difficulty in Richard II. and Henry IV. Here we see a pack of human wolves uniting to remove an obstacle in their way, and then, the immediate object accomplished, viewing each other with distrust and suspicion, which ultimately create the violence they apprehend.

"The love of wicked men converts to fear;
That fear to hate, and hate turns one or both
To worthy danger and deserved death." Richard II. V. i. 66.

Success thus purchased can have no more stability than a wave of the sea.

It is true that in a society altogether dominated by such men, the good are often swept away with the bad to a common ruin. Witness, for instance, the fall of Duke Humphrey, in Henry VI. Nevertheless, there is a tendency at work in favor of the good. In so far as "nobleness enkindles nobleness," they live in a better world than the bad. Brutus could say with his dying breath, J. C.
"In all my life I found no man but he V. v. 34.
was true to me." And thus it proved with Henry V. In contrast with almost all the other reigns of the historical plays, where the king is either self-indulgent and greedy of money, or treacherous and unprincipled, or criminally weak and cowardly, we behold a reign whose peace, as soon as the true temper of the monarch is revealed, is not troubled by a single conspiracy; more than this, a reign in which for the first time in many a year all the subjects of the king rally around him with devotion and enthusiasm in an enterprise that they believe

to be demanded by justice and patriotism. He lived, indeed, in a better world than his father or his son.

The punishment of grave crimes is rendered more certain and also more overwhelming by a principle that is perhaps most effectively exhibited in Macbeth. Only a single act of violence is needed to place the Thane of Cawdor upon the throne of Scotland. But unfortunately circumstances compelled him to make a confidant of one man, Banquo; and who can tell when Banquo may find it to his interest to turn against the master he helped to exalt? So this possible enemy must die. With him must be sacrificed his son, that there may be no avenger left to terrify the murderer, and that the doom announced by the supernatural messengers of fate may be turned aside. These mysterious acts of violence awaken general suspicion and fear. The fear of the subjects awakens new fear in the sovereign, that in turn provokes renewed acts of violence on his part. Strive against necessity as he will, sin, he discovers, plucks on sin; till finally the guilty dupe is buried under their accumulated weight.

As yet, however, we have discovered nothing worthy the name of a universal law. For the penalties thus far enumerated are by no means the inevitable consequence of a violation of the moral order. Some Iagos escape detection, their plans succeed to their entire satisfaction, and they become pillars of society. Even if unmasked, it happens more than once that "the wicked prize itself buys out the law." No exemplification of this truth is more revolting than Henry VIII., whom Shakespeare and Fletcher were compelled to dismiss, secure and apparently happy in the possession of his desired bride, and as the result of his very crimes freed forever from the hateful yoke of Rome. Hamlet III. iii. 59.

What, then, is the successful villain, if only sufficiently callous, after all, a man to be envied? Does his life of unsuspected or at least unchecked crime afford him the expected satisfaction? The answer to this question is given in Macbeth.

If we of the twentieth century would understand the impression made by this great tragedy upon its first auditors, we must become with them for the moment subjects of the first Stuart. We must look back upon the life of our ancestors as cramped and disfigured by conventions, prejudices, and superstitions. We must think of our own life as a thing to be shaped solely with reference to the attainment of the best ends through the use of the most economical means. Whether we happen to know it or not, this ideal has come to us from Italy, where, after the night of the Middle Ages, it blossomed and bore fruit under the regenerating influences of classical culture. The great personalities it produced are not entirely unknown to us. Some were guided by the new light to seek a development of their volitional powers that made them a blessing to their own age and to posterity.

Others there were, however, whose emancipation from the past meant the destruction of every scruple, every restraint that might have kept them from making self the centre of their universe. These latter, if we have caught by contagion, or for any other reason share the feelings of the typical Italian, — these latter are our idols, particularly those among them who have risen to supreme power in the state. In this position they can indulge every wish, yes, every passing whim. What more can life offer? And we could demonstrate, if necessary, that this happy condition would have been forever closed to them, had they not thrust aside from beginning to end every consideration except that of the best means to their own aggrandizement. On the stage, in the seats reserved for the aristocracy, we see the incarnations of our ideals, men who, sometimes from comparatively humble beginnings, have attained to royal favor, wealth, station, and almost boundless power, through their superiority to the considerations that restrain the stupid and timid herd. It is with these thoughts, these ideals in the background of consciousness, that we watch the rise to greatness of a man and a woman dominated by our own spirit. Our hero is not an Italian, as we might have expected. The dramatist has just given us Othello.[1] Perhaps this may have moved him to lay the scene

[1] This chronology is conjectural, as in most cases when we come to details; but, on the whole, it is the most plausible guess we can make.

in another part of the world, and to make the plot turn upon the employment of violence rather than intrigue. Perhaps, too, he thought the majority of his audience could better realize the political conditions of Scotland than of Italy. But whatever may have determined the setting, there can be no mistake about the essence of the drama. It represents the inner life of the unscrupulous and successful political adventurer of the Sixteenth Century.

Macbeth is to-day commonly, perhaps universally regarded as a tragedy of remorse. Such a conception is, I believe, not merely erroneous, it utterly obscures the connection between evil-doing and its harvest that is set forth in the play. The first step towards discovering this relationship must therefore be an examination of the traditional theory.

The view that Macbeth was originally a good man, the only flaw in whose character was a certain lack of determination through which he was led astray by the weird sisters and his wife, this view has fortunately almost disappeared. How it ever came into existence is difficult to understand.

> "What beast was 't, then,
> That made you break this enterprise to me?
> . . . . Nor time nor place
> Did then adhere, and yet you would make both:
> They have made themselves, and that their fitness now

Macbeth I. vii. 47.

Does unmake you. I have given suck, and know
How tender 't is to love the babe that milks me:
I would, while it was smiling in my face,
Have pluck'd my nipple from his boneless gums,
And dash'd the brains out, had I so sworn as you
Have done to this."

Surely these words of Lady Macbeth are sufficiently explicit. The first suggestions of foul play came from Macbeth's own unscrupulous ambition. The rôle of the weird sisters is strictly limited to promising success.

When the time for action finally arrives moral scruples play no part whatever in the hesitation that ensues. Macbeth has found that the thought of murder to be committed in some distant future, and the actual consent of the will to its immediate execution, are quite different things. He is therefore compelled to go through an agony of conflict before he can "bend up each corporal agent to this terrible feat." But the considerations that give him pause are not regard for duty but fear of the "bloody instructions which return to plague the inventor." The world to come, which lies below the horizon line, he is willing to "jump." But he cannot free himself from fear of the vengeance that overtakes in this life the traitor and the murderer. He were resolved, if he could only be assured that the point of his knife would not be turned against himself. True, other and higher considerations enter his mind. For a moment the promptings of honor and loyalty are

I. vii. 1–28.

allowed to hold the attention; thereupon the graces of his sovereign present themselves and prepare to plead for the threatened life. But no, the old familiar counsellors push them aside and hasten to urge the danger to which he will subject himself if he stirs the indignation of his countrymen by outraging their sympathies.

After the crime has been committed the prevailing emotion is not sorrow for sin, but, as before, fear, fear of the dagger and the poisoned cup. It haunts him in his dreams; it drives him to keep a paid agent in every house, and even persuades him to spy upon the cut-throats who do his work; it hounds him on to ever new murders and atrocities. Between the murder of Duncan and the second meeting with the weird sisters fear is the dominant note of every soliloquy and of every dialogue with Lady Macbeth.

I am not unaware that Coleridge finds in these utterances of a troubled mind indications of the activity of conscience.[1] No grounds are alleged for his hypothesis, but in its favor might be urged the fact that Macbeth is a soldier whose bravery and address upon the field of battle had brought him the title and estate of the Thane of Cawdor. This fact, however, proves nothing. Much bravery is merely the insensibility of habit; and use and wont which harden men to danger as they do to privation may leave them helpless in situations that are radically new. Hence the terror with

[1] Notes on Shakespeare: Macbeth.

which ghosts have always inspired even the boldest natures. Coleridge's dictum, in fact, seems to have no other basis than the demands of his own transcendentalism which, discovering no direct traces of moral sensibility proceeds to read them into the text as best it can.

Cf. Macbeth III. iv. 99–106.

Nevertheless, Macbeth is not absolutely without conscience, though Coleridge does not succeed in identifying the indications of its existence. The Scotch nobleman is no mere echo of Richard III. or Iago. In the mouths of neither of these worthies should we hear the words, "For Banquo's issue have I filed my mind;" still less those which follow, "For them the gracious Duncan have I murder'd." It is characteristic of the completely insensible criminal both in the real world and in Shakespeare's representation of it[1] that he looks upon his victim with contempt. Strength is all he admires, and the unsuspecting victim is in his eyes weak and stupid. It is of great significance, therefore, that Macbeth has not lost all his admiration for the childlike innocence of his king even when actually coupled, as it seems to have been in this case, with a lack of force. Equally significant is the farther fact that Macbeth calls his crimes by their proper names, "murder," "treason," "this hangman's [butcher's] hands." For this habit, since it is not the cynicism of the moral imbecile, removes

III. i. 65–66.

[1] Richard III. and Iago.

him from the class of Iago as certainly as it does from that of the half-hardened criminal who in wilful blindness calls theft "purchase."

Nevertheless, Macbeth is a man without real scruples, although faint images of restraining voices sometimes chime upon his inner ear. What moral sensitiveness he possesses is only sufficient to enable him to enjoy coddling himself for his regret at his unfortunate conduct, to make of him a sentimentalizing dealer in fine phrases. He can tell us that treason has done its worst; he can bid seeling night scarf up the tender eye of pitiful day at the very moment when he is completing his arrangements for a second murder. Macbeth's fine phrases about murdering innocent sleep, and the many companion utterances, sound like the musings of a sympathetic and poetically gifted nature who is sitting among the audience and watching the course of the action. Even this puts the case a little too strongly. A love of mouth-filling adjectives and of exaggeration for its own sake appears so frequently that we have to make a double discount upon everything he says. At bottom his sorrow at his own deeds is about as deep and lasting as that of the average play-goer at the misfortunes of last night's heroine. How could it be otherwise in one who believes himself doomed to centuries, probably an eternity, of suffering, yet has so little power to realize the absent that he remains unmoved — certainly undeterred — by the prospect. We ought accordingly to trust

III. ii. 46.

Macbeth no farther than we should Wainewright, the essayist, or Lacenaire, the poet. If he could control his terror he would be able, like Lacenaire, to kill a man with as little compunction as he would drink a glass of wine; and after the murder he would experience as little genuine remorse.

It is not otherwise with Lady Macbeth. The emotions that she drowned in wine were fear that they might fail in their attempt, or be discovered before the traces had been removed. In order to show his newly acquired independence of character, her husband affects to keep from her the murder of Banquo till she may be able to applaud the accomplished deed. She is not so simple as those commentators suppose, who describe her as unable to see what is coming. Nevertheless, she makes no attempt to stay the murderous hand. The only expression of feeling that escapes her after they are started in their career is longing for the lost sense of security.

> "'T is safer to be that which we destroy
> III. ii. 6. Than by destruction dwell in doubtful joy."

If there be any significance in these facts, Lady Macbeth is as bare of moral scruples as is her husband.

It is widely believed that Shakespeare's play as it has come down to us is a torso, possibly wrecked by Middleton, that he might enhance its popularity by restoring it in accordance with the taste of the times. If some such hypothesis be true, we must suppose many passages have been lost that would have thrown additional light upon the heroine's character. But since those we possess unite in telling the same story, we may feel confident that our interpretation correctly represents its main outlines.

This paucity of data, however, has made it possible for another theory to grow up and maintain its ground. According to it, Lady Macbeth is an unselfish and lofty nature, carried away for the moment to do violence to her permanent self by her love for her husband. The evidence for this view will not stand the slightest scrutiny. She loved, we are told, her husband, her father, and her child. Grant this, and nothing is proved. For while strong family affection is not common in the lower grades of criminality, it sometimes occurs.[1] And have we not seen a callous murderer risking his life to save a cat? Her love for her father, of which so much has been made, is certainly not intense enough to have any great effect upon her actions. Possibly we must believe her when she declares,

> "Had he not resembled
> My father as he slept, I had done 't." II. ii. 13.

But this resemblance does not prevent her from placing the daggers where Macbeth cannot miss them; from giving the signal for the deed; from

[1] See above, p. 122.

following her husband's retreating steps with strained attention; from entering a room near the scene she would not witness in order to assure herself of the successful issue. She can even picture the murderer in the very act of striking the blow and at the same time remain calm enough to note that "the surfeited grooms do mock their charge with snores."

Again, her fainting on the discovery that Macbeth has killed the two grooms has been interpreted as an indubitable sign of returning moral sensibility. Let us assume for the sake of argument that the swoon is genuine; that the fact that she needs help at the exact moment when Macbeth begins talking too much is merely a matter of chance. Even so, the conclusion does not follow with necessity, for the incident is susceptible of several different explanations. Macbeth's detailed description of the appearance of the murdered Duncan and the sleeping attendants, perhaps in connection with the disappearance of the effects of the wine, may have awakened her to a realizing sense of her position; and the horror with which it inspired her may have been just that which she sought to banish by the wine.[1]

[1] The following passage from Feuerbach's work, already cited, describes a case so nearly parallel to the swoon of Lady Macbeth as here interpreted, that I cannot refrain from quoting it. Andreas Bichel, a day laborer, lured two young girls into his house and killed them, in order to sell their clothes. At no time after his arrest did he show the slightest trace of remorse; and throughout his examination he maintained his self-control perfectly, except on

To be sure, Lady Macbeth, like her husband, can deal in very effective oratory. Witness the beau-

the occasion to be described. He pleaded not guilty, and as there had been no witnesses of the crime, progress was at first very slow. For a long time the most that could be accomplished was to force him to the admission of one murder, for which the circumstantial evidence was overwhelming. But he so described the conditions that brought it about as to reduce his guilt to a minimum. Finally, in accordance with a Bavarian law framed for such exigencies, he was taken from the town in which the trial was being held to his native village. "He was first brought into the magistrate's office. Immediately upon his entrance he was overcome by the thought that he was now at the place where the crime had been committed, and he was prevented from fainting only by being given some water. The judge addressed him in kind and sensible words: 'You are now,' he said, 'in your native town, near your home and the scene of your crime. Confess the entire truth here and at once. You will be taken to your own home, you will see the corpses themselves.' But the culprit's will still remained stronger than even the powerful feelings that threatened to destroy consciousness. He persisted in the assertion that he knew nothing of the second corpse alleged to have been found in his dwelling.

"Thereupon he was taken to his house. In the principal room lay upon boards the two mangled corpses. He was led to the first one. At this horrible sight he trembled in every limb; the muscles of his face twitched; his expression grew terrible; he demanded water to moisten his lips and mouth. When asked whether he recognized the corpse, he answered in a hollow voice: 'No; I have never before seen a corpse that has lain in the grave.' He was then led to the second one. He could now no longer stand upright, but sank into a chair. His limbs trembled violently and his face was disfigured with hideous contortions. He now declared that he recognized this second body as Katherina Seidel. He was asked to explain his emotion at the sight of the first corpse. 'I trembled only for fear of the people,' was his answer. 'Who would not tremble under circumstances like these?' and persisted in his assertions of ignorance." Feuerbach, *opus cit.*, p. 47.

The emotion that overcame Bichel was fear, as is shown by a study of the entire case. The sight of his native village, then of

I. v. 41. tiful invocation beginning: "Come, you spirits that tend on mortal thoughts." But if this be a picture of a mind really battling with temptation, we must suppose either a very stupid dramatist or a very stupid woman. For if Lady Macbeth had ever learned anything from experience, she must have known that to keep pity from doing its work one must drive it from the mind by the thought of personal gain. The spirits should have been bidden to fill her mind with pictures of that future dignity to which she and her husband aspired, with an imaginative foretaste of the joys of luxury and power. As it stands, therefore, the entire address seems to me to have its source in the same temperament and character that produced her husband's poetic effusions. Outbursts in this vein, to be sure, will hardly be expected from a Goneril, but demonstrably they can come from a Lacenaire. They therefore prove nothing beyond the most rudimentary moral capacity, a capacity just sufficient for a touch of sentimentalism. This particular ebullition does not even indicate a sentimentalism that is innate. As the only piece of declamation in which she is represented as indulging, — unless the remark about her father belongs in the same category,— it perhaps ought to be attributed to the principle that husbands and wives occasionally drop into

his victims, brought home to his imagination for the first time the extent of his danger and the momentousness of the issues in the outcome of his trial.

each other's mannerisms by mere force of imitation. Hence, as soon as the necessity arose of summoning every faculty to the task of toning up the shattered nerves of her companion, she would find no difficulty in throwing aside this loosely worn habit.

The conclusion of the whole matter is that Macbeth and Lady Macbeth are by nature proof against attacks of remorse. Some slight discomfort they may possibly feel for a time, but it will quickly wear off, leaving no trace behind. Armed as they are at this point, will they then escape unscathed in their war against their fellowmen?

The murder of Duncan is in the past. Treason has done its worst. Macbeth is seated upon the throne and Lady Macbeth is queen of Scotland. She has succeeded; her heart's desire is hers. But there is no joy in her soul, for peace has gone forever from her life.

> "Nought 's had, all 's spent,
> Where our desire is got without content:
> 'T is safer to be that which we destroy III. ii. 4.
> Than by destruction dwell in doubtful joy."

We must remember that Lady Macbeth was not a woman of great temperamental courage, as her husband erroneously supposed. Real fearlessness does not need to drink wine in order to make itself bold. It can look fate in the eye, and when the worst presents itself to the imagination it does not recoil with the cry:

II. ii. 33. "These deeds must not be thought
After these ways; so, it will make us mad."

No, she was not insensible to the dangers that surrounded her from the day she entered upon the path of murder. They shook her frame; there were moments, at least, when she thought it better to be dead than bear the agony of an uncertain future. But she possessed a heroic, an almost superhuman will. As long as she could act, even though she had ceased to share altogether the counsels of her lord, she merely suffered, but her emotions did not overthrow her. But when Macbeth had gone into the field, and she was shut up in a castle condemned to inactivity, then the terror that had been locked up within her broke its chains. The mind gave way under the strain of anxiety and the tortured soul exhibited its hitherto hidden agony, not, indeed, in prophecy, but in reminiscence. It is a single theme that we hear when she comes before us for the last time: a little water will *not* clear her of this deed. What then? They will be discovered; and again and again she lives through the fearful scenes in which her husband's weakness threatens to mar all, and her resolution must be the source of his self-control as well as her own. When the knocking at the castle gate broke the silence of the night, when the disordered imagination of her husband conjured up the ghost of

Banquo, she seemed calm and self-possessed. But now we know what storms were sweeping through her mind, what storms have visited it since.

The common opinion that the sleep-walking scene represents the workings of remorse is entirely gratuitous, quite apart from the view we may take of Lady Macbeth's character. A few of its expressions may be so interpreted; none of them must be; a majority cannot be. The dominant note is plainly fear, fear that Macbeth will mar all by his agitation, fear that these hands of hers can never lose the telltale mark of blood. It is noteworthy that Schiller, whose Kantian preconceptions were the only assurance he needed that this must be a representation of remorse, — it is noteworthy that Schiller, when he came to translate this passage, found himself compelled to embody his interpretation in language that has no counterpart in the original. In Shakespeare's text the physician says:

"Foul whisperings are abroad: unnatural deeds
Do breed unnatural troubles: infected minds V. i. 79.
To their deaf pillows will discharge their secrets."

These lines Schiller translates:

"Unnatürlich ungeheure
Verbrechen wecken unnatürliche
Gewissensangst, und die beladne Seele beichtet
Dem tauben Kissen ihre Schuld.

If we read this scene as Shakespeare wrote it, we shall find no evidence of *Gewissensangst.*

The "lesson" to be drawn from Macbeth, therefore, is not that remorse will come; that, as we have seen, will depend upon the development of the moral nature. What is represented is the terror of those who set themselves up as the enemy of mankind. It filled Lady Macbeth's waking thoughts with scorpions, it tortured her nights with timorous dreams. About her is the struggle to keep from her enemies' grasp what she by violence has seized; before her lies the day when one of them will finally succeed. If it be true

M. V. I. i. 75. that "they lose [the world] that do buy it with much care;" if it be true that

Othello III. ii. 173. "riches fineless is as poor as winter to him that ever fears he shall be poor," Lady Macbeth has lost in the game of life. She goes to her death weak, poor, and broken in spirit.

This is no fancy picture, created to frighten the bad and edify the good. Whether it was suggested by the description of the life of the tyrant in Plato's Republic, or by some account of the careers of the famous Italian despots, cannot be determined. At all events, it is a faithful representation of fact. John Addington Symonds writes: "The life of the despot was usually one of prolonged terror. Immured in strong places on high rocks, or confined to gloomy fortresses like the Milanese Castello, he surrounded his person with foreign troops, protected his bed-chamber with a picked guard, and watched his meat and drink lest they should be poisoned. . . . He had no real friends or equals, and against his own family he adopted an attitude of fierce suspicion, justified by the frequent intrigues to which he was exposed. His timidity verged on monomania. Like Alfonso II. of Naples, he was tortured with the ghosts of starved or strangled victims; like Ezzelino, he felt the mysterious fascination of astrology; like Filippo Maria Visconti, he trembled at the sound of thunder,[1] and set one band of body-guards to watch another next his person.[2] He dared not hope for a quiet end. No one believed in the natural death of a prince: princes must be poisoned or poniarded." [3]

But then there are the intrepid. They think all men mortal but themselves, and cannot imagine the dagger as ever reaching them. Cowards may die many times before their death, but they face the inevitable end but once. Success they feel sure of; it is their temperament to be optimistic. Who shall pluck the reward from their hands?

The art of the poet has shown us this, also. Originally, Macbeth was more timorous than his wife. At all events, if he felt no more fear, he had not her art of driving it from the mind when action

[1] Cf. Macbeth: "That I may tell pale-hearted fear it lies,
And sleep in spite of thunder." IV. i. 85.

[2] Cf. Macbeth, Act III., scene iii., line 1 ff. It will not be forgotten that Macbeth, too, was visited by apparitions of the murdered, and that in his terror he resorted to the occult.

[3] The Age of the Despots, p. 118.

was necessary. But he has received supernatural assurance of safety from a source that he never questions. He has, indeed, a war on his hands, but he is a soldier by profession. And has he not been told that he shall never be vanquished until great
IV. i. 92. Birnam wood to high Dunsinane hill
IV. i. 80. shall come against him? and that in
victory or defeat none of woman born shall harm him? Moreover, he has health and the possession of all his faculties, wealth, power, and the assured fame that follows in the train of the kingly office. What lacks he yet?

What lacks he yet? Everything that makes life worth having, for his desire is got without content. Why without content? He knows only too well.

> "That which should accompany old
>   age,
> As honour, love, obedience, troops of
>   friends,
> I must not look to have; but, in their
> V. iii. 24.   stead,
> Curses, not loud but deep, mouth-honour,
>   breath,
> Which the poor heart would fain deny,
>   and dare not."

It was for pomp and power that he gave his soul to the common enemy of man. But the one can permanently amuse only a child; the other he finds an empty word unless the obedience rendered be prompted by loyalty and love. And this he cannot have. For it is the nature of moral evil to divide man from his fellow-man. The egoist thinks he is merely deciding at each point in his career whether he shall snatch this advantage or make that sacrifice. In reality, he is deciding whether he shall lead the broader or the narrower life. With every attack upon others he will grow at the same time more suspicious of his fellows and more indifferent to their interests. If continued, this attitude will extend to his friends, till finally even those he once loved best will become nothing to him except as they are instruments to some ulterior end. Thus he is drawing away from others at the very time when others are drawing away from him, till finally there will come a day when his isolation is complete.

The bitterness of this last stroke was not withheld from Macbeth. Not but that his wife, and possibly some few others, may not have retained till the end their devotion to him. The tragedy of this man's loneliness lay in the fact that he had become incapable of any feeling of unity with them. They were now for him mere walking, gesticulating statues, incapable of speaking to the needs of his soul, and he was alone in this wilderness of lifeless forms. The causes of this final estrangement can, in part, be guessed; in part they must remain forever unknown. Whether it was that prolonged misery had dulled Macbeth's sensibilities, and rendered him incapable of all strong emotion; whether it was that she, who was

Cf. V. v. 9–15.

once nearest to him, had become in his eyes, like the rest, merely a dangerous tool; whether it was that both husband and wife had wakened with a shock, fatal to love, from their illusions respecting each other, — who will venture to say? Certain it is, at all events, that these are not bare abstract possibilities; sooner or later, they must have come. The first two would have been merely the inevitable results of an unbridled egoism, and the conditions into which it had thrust him. The last derives its necessity from the special nature of the relation between Macbeth and Lady Macbeth.

No careful observer can have failed to notice that this man and this woman had never really known each other. Misled by his sonorous phrases, she had thought him too full of the milk of human kindness to catch the nearer way; she had thought him without the wickedness that should attend ambition. Perhaps she was glad to be undeceived. But in the early days of their married life had she expected she would ever, waking or dreaming, have to say, "Fie, my lord, fie! A soldier and afeared"? And can a woman, even the most timorous, and such Lady Macbeth was not, retain her respect for the companion and protector whom she must thus address, not once, but over and over again?

Macbeth, too, had been disillusioned. What can he think of the judgment of the woman who, in the fatal moment of action, had spurred on his will with stinging words? And can he forget that once he had believed her literally invulnerable to fear, and that in a burst of enthusiasm, he had hailed her as one whose "undaunted mettle should compose nothing but males"? I. vii. 73. Now, he finds her strong indeed, but not, as he had fondly imagined, immovably fixed. His respect, or at least his admiration for her, is gone, even as his respect for himself. And his love, be the reasons what they will, has forsaken him, too. He accordingly listens to the tidings of her death with grim indifference: If not at this time, she would have died hereafter; fools are dying every day. V. v. 17–23.

Alas, for Macbeth! Separated as he is from his kind by the prison walls of hatred, with no inspiring ideals, whether of service or character to give content to his life, he feels he has lived long enough. For if this be success, if it is to gain this that men put rancors in the vessel of their peace, then truly

"Life 's but a walking shadow, a poor player
That struts and frets his hour upon the stage
And then is heard no more: it is a tale L. 24.
Told by an idiot, full of sound and fury,
Signifying nothing."

If it had come to this point, the catastrophe that overwhelmed him from without was really a release.

Truly, the wages of Macbeth's sin were death, death in life.

Impressive as is this revelation of the inner life of the fear-free criminal, it will not completely satisfy those who demand an inseparable connection between wickedness and misfortune. For it may with much plausibility be argued that Macbeth's world-weariness and despair were the outcome of an idiosyncrasy of temperament. Such a complete collapse we should expect only where there was an active and unsatisfied longing to receive, and perhaps even to give sympathy. This longing is not incompatible with complete selfishness. It is not infrequently found in the most crassly egoistic, showing itself among other ways in a preference for animal over human companionship; the former being chosen because it involves no serious counter-demands. The existence of this trait in Macbeth is inferable from what I have called his sentimentalizing. His mind in playing with the picture of itself as caring for others, betrays its craving for their interest in its own welfare. But, it may be argued, the hunger for fellowship cannot be a necessary constituent of human nature. In some men it appears to be non-existent; in others, rudimentary. Is not this appearance fact?

Problems of possibilities, it must be obvious, do not belong within the province of the drama, whose function it is to mirror certain, necessarily narrow, areas of the existent. We may infer with much plausibility, however, that Shakespeare considered the desire for sympathy an all but universal phenomenon, appearing often like subterranean streams in the most unpromising places. He found it in a man like Richard III.:

> "I shall despair. There is no creature loves me:
> And if I die, no soul shall pity me."

Richard III. V. iii. 200.

He found it in Gloucester's ruthless son:

> "Yet Edmund was beloved!"

Lear V. iii. 239.

This hunger may be forgotten in the first enthusiasm over some newly won success; but in the barren days between great events, most of all in the periods of depression and failure that spare no man, it will return. These few touches of the artist's brush, then, are a revelation of the bitterness of soul that overwhelms the base mind when the future looks black, when losses crowd upon him, when failure has laid upon him her iron hand. In these gloomy hours the unselfish may turn to extra-personal interests. The satisfaction of these will give content to their lives. But for the self-centred there is only unsatisfied craving.

But however wide-spread the desire for human fellowship may be, Shakespeare seems to teach that it may occasionally fail. In Iago, for instance, there is no trace of it. He knows nothing of family affection, of mutual confidences, helpfulness, and brotherhood; of delight in the service either of his general or the state. So much joy, of course, he can never possess. On the other hand, its absence does not appear to distress him in the least. Has he not, then, escaped his punishment? May he not find life, on the whole, a very comfortable affair?

The answer to this question has not been left to conjecture. Iago's mind harbors an inmate as sombre as discontent. The cynicism of this ruthless intriguer is not the active despair of virtue which we find in Hamlet, for apart from the fact that he has no love for it, he believes in its existence here and there, and counts upon it as one of the strings by which to pull his marionettes. His cynicism is rather contempt for the race as a herd of fools, often weak and always stupid, a contempt that has its source partly in the consciousness of his own powers, partly in his incapacity to look with sympathetic vision into the inner palpitating life of his less clever fellow-men. Nothing but warm and deep sympathies can save the superior person — or him who supposes himself such — from a distaste for his human environment as for the monotonous sandy flats of a vast desert, in the midst of which fate has imprisoned him. For through the sympathies alone is revealed the significance and worth of that mingling of nobility and weakness, insight and error, struggle and torpor, joy and sorrow, that form the content of the commonplace life. Iago's every word and deed testify to this corroding bitterness of soul. His existence is thus an essentially joyless one, lightened as it is only by an occasional gleam of satisfaction at his own acuteness and strength of will.

If Iago had been dull of intellect he might, of course, have escaped this experience — at what cost I need hardly point out. Intellectual mediocrity accompanied by emotional and volitional barrenness has perhaps never attracted even the most superficial amateur in the art of living. Confining our attention, then, to the selfishness of intellectual endowment, we discover that an inexorable fate seems to have set before it these alternatives: the isolation of an unsatisfied longing for human fellowship; the isolation of cynical contempt. The former, we are distinctly taught, will poison and reduce to less than nothingness the most brilliant outward success. Whether the latter finds adequate compensation in power, station, and luxury, has been left for the spectator to determine. If he agrees with the estimate placed upon them by those Shakespearean characters who have learned their value from personal experience, his problem will not be difficult.

The preceding study of the relation between wickedness and its harvest has brought before us the principal factors involved, in so far as Shakespeare has described them. Whether there may not be some loop-hole through which guilt occasionally escapes, especially where it is commingled with a certain share of goodness, an inquiry that confines itself to his text cannot undertake to decide. What it can and does show is the nature of the most important tendencies at work, and the insignificance of the chance in favor of their neutralization.

Our result is no copy-book morality, no smug assurance, Be good and you will be happy. The gentle Desdemona, all love, all service; Horatio bending over the body of his dead friend; Kent broken upon the wheel to which his devotion has bound him, — these are not happy. The leap from the principle that moral enthusiasm is, at its highest, a *conditio sine qua non* of happiness to the principle that it is a sufficient condition of happiness is so violent that it could hardly escape the attention of any unbiased observer. Accordingly, I should not think of giving a moment's consideration to such a doctrine if it had not been either tacitly assumed or expressly asserted by certain very "profound thinkers," and in particular by certain "profound" Shakespearean critics.

For one who is willing to see things as they are, there can be no question of the fundamental value of a well-endowed intellect, especially in stirring times and in highly organized societies. Not only are the specific joys of the intellectual life, including the consciousness of intellectual power, forever closed to those who stand no higher than a Chinese coolie; it is equally certain that tact, — one-half of which is sagacity, — keenness of observation, retentiveness of memory, and power of analysis and of inference, must be ranked among the important instruments for the attainment of the various goods of life. In Shakespeare's transcript, their part is nowhere minimized. In the success of Henry V. and the failure of Brutus; in the mistakes of Cordelia and the misfortunes of Edgar and Gloucester; in the tragic blindness of Othello; yes, in the wreck of Timon's faith, defects of intellect are fully as potent as sins of will.

Nor is there any refusal, at least in the great masterpieces, to acknowledge the rôle of that incalculable and intractable factor that men call chance. Its range, to be sure, is reduced to a minimum; but such treatment would be demanded under any circumstances by the principles of dramatic art. The function of tragedy is to awaken awe (not fear, as Aristotle taught) and pity. Somewhere within the length and breadth of human life we must therefore be brought into the presence of power. And of this the intellect and the will of man are the chief seat. Still more impressive, however, even though it terrify, is the revelation of power that we behold in those unbending resistless laws of life that enfold man and bear him onward to destruction. Before the sweep of these mighty energies the accidental must be kept in the background. Accident, to be sure, is not lawless. But it is the product of a confluence of forces, the necessity for which usually cannot be seen, or at least realized. Furthermore, the accidental, as that which is occasional, lacks the massiveness which gives power much of its hold upon the imagination. Tragedy, therefore, must use chance sparingly. But while Shakespeare minimizes to the utmost the influence of this factor, he does not and cannot entirely conceal it. The aged Lear craves love and sympathy. No one can help remembering that marriage with a different wife might have given him affectionate daughters, and that, as it is, if death had taken Goneril and Regan in their infancy, the old king never would have seen his train disquantitied, or been driven out into the night and storm. Illustrations of the principle are numberless. Consider one more. Not even an Alfred or a St. Louis is perfect. Evidently whether the flaw in their characters shall be fatal or relatively harmless will depend upon circumstances. This appears with perfect clearness in Othello. Shakespeare has used every resource at his command to make Othello's fate the outcome of his character. His suspicions of Desdemona's unfaithfulness do not turn upon the chance loss of a handkerchief or the casual meeting of Cassio and Bianca. They spring from the hot impetuosity he drew from his barbaric ancestors. But these deadly forces might have remained quiescent forever if he had not hitherto been surrounded by honorable men, if he had known something of women except by hearsay, or if Iago had

Cf. III. iii. 333–479.

taken service with Genoa rather than Venice. They might have been shut up in harmlessness had the Turkish fleet come down upon Cyprus and thus given Desdemona and Cassio time to clear themselves. Even an accidental delay of five minutes in the commission of the murder might have brought the explanation that would have prevented the catastrophe.

Life, as Mr. Spencer has taught us, is an adjustment of inner to outer relations. Thus it is possible for the external factor, which we have been calling chance, to take the precedence in determining individual fate. Shakespeare's one illustration of this in the field of tragedy is the youthful work, Romeo and Juliet. But in bringing danger and trial to a happy termination he does not hesitate to show what it can do. In All 's Well that Ends Well the virtues of Helena would have had no room in which to work, had it not been for a series of very unusual though doubtless possible accidents. In Cymbeline the lovers, and in The Winter's Tale parents and daughter, are restored to each other by a chain of circumstances that genius and heroism could never by themselves have forged. While, if any concatenation of chances could be appropriately used as an illustration for the text, "Fortune brings in some boats that are not steer'd," it would be the disclosure of the intrigue in Much Ado about Nothing through the collision, so to speak, between loquacity and simplicity under the dripping eaves of

Cym. IV. iii. 46.

Leonato's palace. In life as in whist, what is given from without has a part in the result.

The only way to avoid this conclusion is to maintain, with Job's friends, that the fortunate are really the righteous (nowadays they call themselves "the fittest"), the unfortunate are really the wicked. This style of exegesis, when applied to the minor characters of Macbeth, for instance, leads us to such conclusions as the following: "The gracious Duncan falls, obviously not without being himself to blame for his fate, for whether the numerous revolts against his government, in the suppression of which Macbeth proved his heroism, were the result of arbitrary rule and injustice, or (as the source from which Shakespeare drew his subject has it) of unroyal weakness and concession, still, he is open to the reproach of not having properly fulfilled his duties as king. His sons are suspected of having slain their father, owing to their precipitate flight, which, though prudent, was unmanly, and have, therefore, to suffer banishment. Banquo, in self-complacent conceit, believes in the promises for his future good fortune, and thus brings destruction upon his own head. Macduff's wife and children, lastly, suffer for the thoughtlessness of their natural protector, who, in thinking only of himself, and forgetful of his duty as father and husband, leaves them behind to secure his own safety. He is punished by their death, which at the same time is Lady Macduff's punishment for the unloving asperity with which she rails at her husband's conduct, and thus gives us an insight into a marriage which was perhaps also a motive for Macduff's hasty and secret flight."[1] Examining this formidable list of casualties it will be impossible for the reader who has reached middle life to refrain from feeling highly flattered at finding himself alive.[2]

The preceding justification of the ways of Shakespeare with his characters is the fruit of German thoroughness. But the greatest achievement in this manner must be set down to the credit of Missouri. The untimely death of Desdemona is commonly looked upon as presenting some difficulties to the good-happy theory of life. Some thinkers have explained it by pointing out that she told fibs ; others have reminded us that she disobeyed her father. But such considerations are either ignored or brushed aside by the St. Louis critic, for he has a profounder thought. The crime of Desdemona, he tells us, consisted in marrying a man of a different

[1] Hermann Ulrici, Shakespeare's Dramatic Art, Book IV. chap. iv. English translation by L. Dora Schmitz, Vol. I., p. 474.

[2] The most ingenious part of this critique is undoubtedly the punishment of Macduff through the death of his children. Readers of John G. Saxe may remember a parallel case. Hoho of the Golden Belt was a high-born Chinese who murdered seven wives in succession on grounds of financial exigencies. Having been detected in his last venture, he was condemned by an unfeeling judge to be hanged. But through the interposition of his friends his punishment was graciously commuted by the Emperor to the decapitation of his three brothers, and the beating of his slaves three times a day for a month.

race.[1] In fairness to Mr. Snider I ought to add that he does not for a moment suppose that the gentle Desdemona meant the least harm in the world. But he thinks that they who unwittingly ally themselves with the powers of evil must expect the same fate as the conscious seekers after wickedness. Possibly they must. But if right and wrong depend upon the intention, this is an arrangement which our sense of justice can never call moral. In fact, when Job's friends are reduced to such straits as this, they have practically given up their case.

It is obvious whither our study has been leading us. Happiness requires the co-operating activity of two factors. The first is the desire or taste within; the second is the means of satisfying or meeting it, which in the last analysis are supplied directly or indirectly by the physical or social environment. Accordingly the question of happiness can no more be decided by confining attention to the former condition alone than it can by an examination of the latter. However, the environment commonly supplies a certain minimum of material. In such cases deep and wide-spreading moral and, if possible, intellectual interests, united with the patience, self-control, and skill to make the most out of our store, afford an apparent independence of externals, and thus promise a happiness that no storm shall be able to sweep away. This promise will be fulfilled in the great majority of instances.

[1] Denton J. Snider, System of Shakespeare's Dramas, Vol. I. p. 104 ff.

But we cannot lay down a universal law, for there is a mysterious exception. Shakespeare has shown us that there is a condition in which no internal worth, no gift of genius, no harmonious adjustment of outer resources to inner needs and wishes can avail to give contentment or inspire the desire to see to-morrow's sun.

The representation of this fact we owe to the difficulties in which the poet involved himself by his habit of using as material for his plots old stories that had caught the popular fancy. Of all preposterous fabrications that he ever deigned to employ, those that form the basis of the Merchant of Venice are the most absurd; and among these the prize for inanity must certainly be awarded to the story of the pound of flesh. It assumes that an experienced man of affairs, possessing a credit that would have given him his choice of terms, accepts a loan from a money-lender whose obvious aim in the transaction is to get a chance to murder him by due process of law. Or, if this interpretation be rejected on the ground that Antonio would naturally suppose he would have no difficulty in paying off the debt, the assumption must be that a thoroughly honorable man enters into an arrangement by which he plans to obtain a loan without interest from an acknowledged enemy.

We are furthermore required to believe that as the report of one disaster follows upon another, this practical business man neither makes an effort to communicate with his friend a few miles distant

— who in his new-found happiness has forgotten his benefactor, — nor consults a lawyer, nor (apparently) makes any attempt to borrow money from professional money lenders or from the brother merchants whom he had himself so often assisted. We may indeed suppose that he approached his friends and was unsuccessful, as Timon was; but this hypothesis would introduce a tragic element into the drama which I think lay outside of the intention of the poet. Besides, it would not help in the least. For it is absurd to suppose that no money lender could be found, if not in Venice, then elsewhere, who could be induced to lend him a comparatively small sum — fifty thousand dollars in present values — at a rate of interest high enough to cover the risk. Even this is not a complete statement of the absurdities of the situation, but I forbear.

These manifold difficulties are overcome by a device than which nothing simpler could be imagined. Antonio is represented at the opening of the play as overclouded with a profound melancholy. He is weary of life, and cares nothing to draw out a joyless existence to a greater length. He has too much principle to deliberately seek death; but if chance will have him killed then chance may kill him. The situation, it may be remembered, recurs in As You Like It,
I. ii. 195–205. and again in Cymbeline, a fact that will
V. i. 22–33; iii. 66–83. not surprise the reader who has noticed
the frequency with which a device is

repeated that has once proved effective. I must add that the idea need not have been original with Shakespeare. If he had read Montaigne's Essays either in the original or in the unpublished manuscript of Florio's translation, he may have been familiar with the passage in which the acute Frenchman, echoing, no doubt, a suggestion of Xenophon, clears up a somewhat similar incident which has occasioned much perplexity. "In observing the wisdom of Socrates and many circumstances of his condemnation," writes Montaigne, "I should dare to believe that he himself, by collusion, in some measure purposely contributed to it; fearing by a longer life, he having then reached his seventieth year, to see his lofty mind and universal knowledge cramped and stupefied by old age."[1]

In converting the string-pulled puppet of the Italian story into a living creature of flesh and blood, Shakespeare has done more than supply one of his characters with an intelligible motive for walking into an open trap; he has negatived — whether he knew it or not — the universality of a certain theory of life. Antonio has wealth, friends, social and business position, and an outlet for his energies through commercial transactions that carry his thoughts to the four corners of the world. He impresses us as being a man of culture, and his generosity to all that needed help in Venice speaks of a life enriched by the enthusiasm of humanity.

[1] Essays, Book III., chap. ii., *sub fin.*

By all the rules, he ought to be happy; yet he is sad and knows not why. We attempt to explain this mysterious fact by a reference to temperament, a word which, in the main, marks our ignorance. But this we do know: with some, unmotived melancholy is a companion through life; with others, as Antonio, it comes without warning from a clear sky, and may again as unexpectedly disappear. Where it abides, intellectual endowment, cultivated tastes, and character, are as powerless to produce real joy in existence as is wealth or any other stock target of the conventional moralist.

In facing this fact, the correlative truth will, of course, not be forgotten. There are men of small intellectual and moral calibre, harassed, it may be, by financial troubles or ill-health, stripped of friends through the incursions of death, whose cheerfulness, nevertheless, flows on like a great river. The barren lands through which they journey glow with a light that comes all from within. And as they look back upon what we should call life's rough and lonely way, they declare they would gladly travel the same road a second time. Such persons do not appear in Shakespeare's plays, for he has no room for detailed studies of commonplace men or commonplace lives. Falstaff we cannot consider an example; for, apart from other objections, he seems to be gay rather than happy. Perhaps the nearest approach to the type is the rogue, Autolycus, in The Winter's Tale. But he is nothing more than a sketch; so that whether his jokes and his songs stand for mere gayety, or for childlike, unmotived joy in being alive, we cannot determine. The sunshine in the faces of the best among the southern negroes of the last generation shows how little in the way of outer accessories or inner resources these natures require.

Out of the complicated mass of details that have passed before our view, the law of the correlation between character and welfare emerges with unmistakable clearness. Evil-doing tends to loss, reckoning values as even the evil-doer himself would estimate them. Even where the result is not "outer" failure, we may expect to find a life poor in compelling and satisfying interests, bare of enthusiasm, haunted by a sense of isolation. On the other hand, the tendency of virtue is exactly the reverse, if by virtue be understood active devotion to moral ideals, and not the mere frigid respectability that is content with a negative stainlessness. Other things being equal, the man vivified and inspired by these ideals will attain success where the evil-minded and the lukewarm miscarry. And even when the success that the crowd struggles for is missed, or when fortune checkers the journey with suffering and disappointment, other tendencies are at work in his favor. In so far as he habitually dwells within the circle of other men's lives, his sorrows are divided, his joys multiplied; and his interests, by their mere extent, assume a fixity and a security unknown to him who risks his all in a single ship. However, here, as in the case of health, culture, and every other good, we can speak of nothing more inevitable than tendencies. In the intricate, close-woven web of life no thread runs straight. The conjunction is more nearly universal, however, for wickedness than for virtue, because it requires a smaller combination of conditions to make us miserable than to make us happy. Thus it comes about that the laws which link consequences with conduct are more easily discoverable in the life of a criminal than in the life of a saint.

In the commentary of Gervinus we may read that Richard III. came to grief "in consequence of the merited justice and due punishment of God." This seems to mean that he was cut off by an arbitrary interference with the order of things on the part of an external omnipotent Agency. That doctrine was not derived from the text. For the gory drama that came from the hands of the youthful Shakespeare distinctly teaches that, given man as he is, it lies in the very nature of moral evil to react upon the perpetrator with effects similar in kind to those which issue from his own will. And as the young dramatist gains in power and insight, and the human world in its completeness begins to take form under his magician's wand, he shows that the laws which make the evil-doer "merely
All's Well his own traitor" depend upon the in-
IV. iii. 25. most constitution of man as a social being; that they hold, whatever view we may take of human origin or destiny; that they no more

need regulation from without to assure their continued working than do the laws of physiology; that we are not called upon to have faith in them, but have only to shake ourselves free from the mental sluggishness into which we allow ourselves to sink, and see them for ourselves.

It is now possible to answer, in part, at least, the third of the great problems forced upon our attention by the phenomena of moral imbecility.[1] To the conscienceless, the good man's ideals of conduct necessarily seem absurd and contemptible, the good man a stupid weakling. Dostoieffsky writes of a noted bandit, a fellow-convict with him in his Siberian prison: "I tried once or twice to speak to Orloff about his exploits; this was evidently a sore point with him, but nevertheless he always answered me readily. But when it dawned upon him that I was appealing to his conscience, his whole manner changed at once; he stared at me with an expression of mingled pride, contempt, and even pity, as if I had suddenly become in his eyes a miserable, silly little boy, to whom he could not talk as he would have done to a grown-up man. A moment later he burst into a good-humored laugh, and I am afraid that he may often have laughed at the remembrance of my words."[2] It is in this spirit that the royal brigand, Richard III., adds to the blessing of his mother the ironical epilogue, "and make me die a good old man." It is possible, we see, to meet **Richard III. II. ii. 109.**

[1] See above, p. 131.

[2] Buried Alive, chap. iv.

contempt with contempt, and if Albany may say to Goneril, "Wisdom and goodness to the vile seem vile," it will be quite in her spirit to reply: "Wisdom and goodness to the milk-livered and the servile seem absurdly important matters." Who, then, is right, or are both equally right, each from his own point of view?

Lear IV. ii. 38.

Cf. Dionyza in Pericles IV. iii. 49–51.

Contempt is the reaction upon supposed weakness, whether of intellect or of will. That perfection of character means not weakness of will but power has already been shown.[1] That the evil-doer who kills his better impulses is an intellectual weakling should now be evident. For if it is the part of wisdom to guide oneself by probabilities, then the evil-doer in choosing the worse has taken the foolish part. I do not say he will discover that he might have done better. What he will find is that the world is a dreary place for such as he, and its promises lies. Meanwhile those he calls fools have placed themselves in the way of obtaining the good gifts which wait for those who are warm of heart and strong of will. Compare the career of Henry V. with that of his father; compare the life of Prospero with that of Iago. The former in each case contains not merely more to admire but, quite apart from the joy of possessing the admirable, more to satisfy. Moral laws, then, possess at least this much objectivity: they are the

[1] See above, p. 18 ff.

laws of both individual and social welfare in the widest sense of the term. Whether they possess or indeed require objectivity in any other sense is a problem that lies beyond the boundaries of our inquiry.

CHAPTER VIII

ETHICS AND METAPHYSICS

WE have now completed our survey of the moral life so far as Shakespeare can serve as guide. But our studies, especially our studies in crime, have left us with problems more tremendous and, to many persons, more insistent than any we have as yet considered. The world-old perplexities about non-moral and moral evil, — failure, and suffering, and wickedness, — have forced themselves upon our attention and press for solution.

The place and function of evil in the world is a subject that evidently lies outside the sphere of descriptive ethics. We may talk glibly — and correctly, too, — about adjustment to the needs of existence. But why, we must go on to inquire, were not the conditions of existence so arranged that those fitted for survival should be at the same time fitted to live a thoroughly satisfactory life, and to play their part in a perfect social order. To answer such questions we must know the purpose of the universe, or whether it really has a purpose. We must know whether this passing life is a part of a larger whole. Most of all we must know whether there is a Providential government of the world. We are learning that all is law: may we believe with similar confidence that all is love? If this great question can only be answered in the affirmative we can let the other puzzles go. The solutions of the problem of evil offered from time to time by "God's spies" may make us smile; but faith will now serve instead of knowledge, and we shall feel that we can afford to wait. Thus does ethics lead up to the supreme problem of metaphysics. Thus does our own study lead up to the question: What does Shakespeare teach about the nature of ultimate reality?

If we think it worth while to attempt an answer to this question we must realize that our inquiry has been given a different direction from that which it has been following in the preceding chapters. There we were studying the results of the dramatist's observations. What generalizations he formed on the basis of the material he collected, or whether he sought to classify and arrange it at all, did not concern us in the least. Here, on the other hand, the man behind the work is everything. What he thought about an order of reality inaccessible to observation has become the object of investigation.

Since the days of Kant it has been generally agreed that all metaphysics must rest upon a theory of knowledge. That is to say, before attempting a solution of the problem of the nature and constitution of the supersensible, we must take stock of our intellectual resources, must ask ourselves whether there are means at our disposal for accomplishing our purpose. In like manner we shall do well to preface our own special inquiry with a few prolegomena to every future system of dramatic hermeneutics. We must ask how a writer of plays can disclose his views on matters metaphysical, provided he makes use of no medium of expression but the stage. Lack of thought on this subject has been the ruin of many a beautiful system of Shakespearean theology.

The first device which suggests itself is that employed by Goethe in Faust. The play opens, we remember, with a prologue in heaven that shall justify the ways of God with the tempted and erring seeker for life's *summum bonum;* it closes with the reception into Paradise of the same soil-stained traveller, who through his many wanderings had been ever dimly conscious of the direction of his goal. But this very example shows how fallacious may be any inference from the creation to the mind of the creator. Only in the vaguest and most shadowy fashion do the introduction and conclusion of Faust represent Goethe's beliefs. And it is not essentially inaccurate to maintain that these scenes meant neither more nor less to him than did the Norse mythology to the composer of the Ring des Nibelungen. Hence, when we see the supersensible represented upon the stage we are bound to ask first, what is its artistic significance, or what facts of this life does it symbolize? Furthermore, the dramatist knows we must ask it. If it have such significance, if it symbolize non-metaphysical truths, we have no criterion for determining how much is creed and how much is art.

The application of this principle to our own problem is obvious. On the wind-swept platform before the Castle of Elsinore appears a visitor from another world. What does this apparition mean? At least this much: though one rise from the dead, Hamlet cannot be moved to action. A short time will pass and the impression that made his brain reel will have retained only so much force as to make him uneasy in his inactivity. Within a week, or possibly a fortnight, a gentleman of Normandy will arrive in Denmark, bringing remarkable reports from Paris of Laertes' skill with the rapier. At once emulation will suggest to Hamlet a welcome substitute for duty. And from that time forth, while his father's spirit is waiting impatiently for the promised vengeance, he will spend his days in continuous practice to become the equal of a careless young gallant in swordsmanship.[1] This midnight vision thus tells us nothing

[1] These facts are obtained by comparing Act IV., scene vii., ll. 71–106, the dialogue between the king and Laertes, with what Hamlet himself says to Horatio in Act V., scene ii., l. 220. The time can be determined in either of two ways. First from Hamlet's words: "Since [Laertes] went into France I have been in continual practice." Laertes left Denmark on the same day on which the dead king's ghost appeared to Hamlet. Second: Laertes and the king form their plot against Hamlet's life within a very short time after the presentation of the Murder of Gonzago by the players. This was four months after King Hamlet's death, as appears from Act III., scene ii., l. 136. The interval between the death of the king and the interview upon the castle platform, was a

of Shakespeare's beliefs about a life beyond the grave. For whether it be thought to represent in itself fact or fancy, it belongs where it is in virtue of its artistic effectiveness and the revelation it affords of Hamlet's character.

There is, however, one way in which a dramatist can stamp unequivocally his confession of faith upon the products of his imagination. That doughty old gladiator, Ben Jonson, never left auditor or reader in a moment's doubt about certain of his metaphysical views. That he regarded atheism as a contemptible hypothesis, and that he rejected totally the puritan theory of salvation, are witnessed by the abuse heaped at every turn upon the adherents of these doctrines. A thoroughly objective dramatist, however, would be incapable of such enormities. Shakespeare, for instance, never permits one character after another to indulge in wholesale abuse of any class of men, except in the case of the "mob." And even the unpleasant impression left in our minds by the wearisome girding at the many-headed multitude is mitigated by the sympathy uniformly exhibited in his treatment of the humble and commonplace individuals whose coming together forms its substance.

Theological beliefs Shakespeare never attacks through their adherents. It is, indeed, quite gener-

little less than two months (see Act I., scene ii., l. 138). If, therefore, we subtract the two months that have elapsed since the arrival of the Norman (IV., vii., 82,) we can hardly date it at a point more than a fortnight removed from the night on which Hamlet received his commission.

ally supposed that in Malvolio and Angelo puritanism is held up to ridicule and contempt. But no assumption could be more arbitrary. Angelo is not an ordinary hypocrite, as is often asserted. He is a man who thinks himself a servant of conscience, whereas in reality he is merely a slave of respectability. The possession of unlimited power reveals his true character to himself as it does to the world. But were he Tartuffe himself, it would not follow that some one else must be a whited sepulchre. Least of all that the doctrines of predestination and absolute decrees must be false. Malvolio, again, is drawn without a trace of bitterness. It would make no difference even if he were not, for he is declared not to be a puritan. "Sometimes he is a kind of puritan," says the sharp-tongued Maria. "O, if I T. N. II.
thought that, I'ld beat him like a dog!" iii. 151.
replies Sir Andrew Aguecheek. Indeed, the traditional view as to the tendency of this piece of characterization turns the facts topsy-turvy. For surely if to be pilloried by a fool is the highest form of praise, no eulogy upon a religious sect could have been more flattering than Sir Andrew's abuse.

A dramatist, however, might make use of another device for presenting his own metaphysical views. He could exhibit them as the beliefs of his best and wisest characters. This does not differ in principle from Ben Jonson's method, but in actual operation it is at least compatible with decency.

According to what seems to be at present a widespread opinion, Shakespeare availed himself of this device. And if we may believe some intelligent men who claim to have either read or seen the plays, he used it to recommend theological and metaphysical agnosticism. Waiving for the present the more general assertion, let us consider the proposition that Shakespeare's most completely rounded characters are skeptics.

This statement, in the form in which it usually appears, can be shown to be baseless. Brutus — to begin with the opening play of the third period — seems to have shared with the contemporaneous Stoics their uncertainty about a future life. But we have no ground to question his confession of faith in "a providence of some high powers that govern us below." To be sure, a false conception of honor does not permit him to act upon it in the decisive matter of taking his life. But in this respect he differs not at all from many a duellist of a later age, nor, indeed, from the high-minded Hector, who also, as may be remembered, prefers the good opinion of others before an acknowledged duty.

J. C. V. i. 107.

The reputation of Hamlet as the typical doubter, the imaginative incorporation of the spirit of Montaigne, is one of the most extraordinary vagaries of Shakespearean criticism. Here is a man whose fate turns upon a visit from a disembodied spirit; a man who is expected by his father to count it a double wrong for the victim of assassination to be cut off in the midst of his sins, with no chance to purge his soul by the ministrations of the priest; a man who fears no ghost, because he can say:

> "And for my soul, what can it do to that,
> Being a thing immortal as itself?"

Hamlet I. iv. 66.

a man who, when the opportunity to discharge his commission thrusts itself upon him, succeeds in disguising to himself his own unwillingness to take the irrevocable step by the consideration that to kill one engaged in prayer is to send his soul to a better world; a man so completely dominated by the religious view of life that he falls into the error of mistaking the results of his own insight for the miraculous interference of Providence in his behalf. Truly, a skeptic of this kind would have little to fear from the fires of the Inquisition.

III. iii. 73–95.

Cf. III. iv. 202–210, IV. ii. 12–23, IV. iii. 50, with V. ii. 4–11.

What, then, lies upon the other side? Nothing but an ambiguous phrase or two in the great soliloquy of Act III. "To be, or not to be:" I have known intelligent men who understand this as the expression of a doubt about immortality. As a matter of fact, the context shows that Hamlet is here dallying with the thought of suicide. "To sleep: perchance to dream." Immortality, we are told, is here presented as nothing more than a bare possibility. Such, indeed, is the most natural

III. i. 56.

L. 65.

interpretation of these five words when isolated from their context. And although the effect of the "perchance" seems to be neutralized by the subsequent treatment of the possibility as a factor sufficiently important to determine the direction of action, yet it must be confessed that the passage does not seem easy to harmonize with the explicit declarations of other portions of the text. Two explanations of the phrase are possible. One is that for the moment Shakespeare had forgotten Hamlet, and was bodying forth his own world-weariness, his own doubts, and fears, and longings for release. As the commentators have pointed out, there is much to commend this view. For instance, complaints about

> "The law's delay,
> L. 72. The insolence of office and the spurns
> That patient merit of the unworthy takes,"

sound rather oddly in the mouth of a prince, unless we suppose him to be taking an exceptionally objective view of the evils of life. And,
L. 79. "the undiscover'd country from whose bourn no traveller returns," still remains, after all the ingenuity that has been expended upon it, an inappropriate expression for one who has seen his father rise from the grave. This hypothesis is thus not without some plausibility. But since its acceptance would involve us in the inconclusive controversies of Shakespearean biography, we ought to try to get along without it. This seems perfectly

possible. For the difficulties disappear if we assume that there are two Hamlets: the one confident as a parish priest of the truth of his religion; the other a student of the world's thought, who sometimes rubs his eyes in uncertainty whether his beliefs are dream or substance. The basis on which this hypothesis rests is far from being an impossibility. Some of the most thoroughly convinced Christians know moments of darkness, when the foundations of religious faith seem to be crumbling beneath their feet. We shall hardly count Alfred Edersheim a theological skeptic. Yet he makes this confession: "Let no one dare to say that the faith of John the Baptist failed, at least till the dark waters have rolled up to his own soul. For mostly all and each of us must pass through some like experience; and only our own hearts and God know how death-bitter are the doubts, whether of head or of heart, when question after question raises, as with devilish hissing, its head, and earth and heaven seem alike silent to us."[1] Unless the dramatist has deceived us, such moods were but occasional in Hamlet. His prevailing attitude was one of faith.

Not to weary the reader with more details to the same effect, we may pass on to the last of the "skeptics," namely Prospero. Every school-boy knows the lines ending, "our little life is rounded with a sleep." This, it is **Tempest IV. i. 157.**

[1] Alfred Edersheim, The Life and Times of Jesus the Messiah. Vol. I., p. 667.

asserted, can mean only that death ends all. If so, St. Luke must have been denying the immortality of the soul when, in describing the stoning of Stephen, he wrote: "When he had said this he fell asleep."[1] When we speak of sleep we may think of the awakening after unconsciousness, or of the unconsciousness itself. Common fairness, therefore, ought to make us admit that Prospero's words are wholly ambiguous. With the recognition of this fact there remains but one passage that even promises a clue to his beliefs about the super-
I. ii. 159. sensible world. "We came ashore," he tells Miranda, "by Providence divine." But again hope fails. For you may interpret this as meaning just what it says, or you may assume that Prospero was talking down to Miranda because she was young and a woman. Whichever alternative you choose, you will discover nothing in the rest of the play to disturb your convictions.

We have assured ourselves, I trust, that we have no right to set down Shakespeare's best characters as uniformly skeptics. From this statement it may perhaps be inferred that they agree in holding certain positive theological and metaphysical doctrines. This is a point that we shall proceed to investigate.

The most prominent heroic figure of the second period of Shakespeare's dramatic career is Henry V. As Prince Hal he is a boy, and nothing more; but as king he represents devotion to

[1] Acts vii., 60.

God and joyful trust in Him, carried to the highest point attainable by the active temperament. This, it may be objected, was in the chronicle. So was much else that is rigorously excluded, as his unpitying persecution of the Lollards and the plots to which it gave rise. Shakespeare used the chronicles as Michael Angelo the quarries of Carrara; he looked them over and took what suited his purpose. We must recognize, therefore, that it is by deliberate choice that Henry V. is presented as profoundly convinced of the truth of the fundamental doctrines of Christian theology.

The first great figures of the third period are Brutus and Hamlet. Brutus, we remember, exhibits belief in a providential government of the world, but he seems to have little or no faith in immortality. We hear nothing from him of a meeting with his friend in a future life, when anticipation would certainly have found expression. Hamlet, too, believes in a divinity that shapes our ends; he believes his soul immortal. But there are moods in which life after death is little more than a "perchance."

As we proceed the clouds grow blacker. A short time after the appearance of Hamlet, as most authorities agree, Measure for Measure was put on the stage. Its principal male character, the Duke of Vienna, must be considered, I think, a doubter or a positive disbeliever in a God of love and in immortality, in spite of an isolated **M. for M.**
utterance which on the surface seems **V. i. 485-7.**

to indicate the contrary.[1] For when called upon to prepare Claudio for his supposed impending death he has no better consolation to offer than the prospect of deliverance from the evils of this life. There he stands in the guise of a priest; the culprit before him believes in a life after death, for he shrinks back from the horrors of purgatory. Yet the duke can tell nothing of the grace of God, or the joys of heaven. He can only point to life as a thing that none but fools would keep, III. i. 5-41. and death as a release from a painful, meaningless treadmill.

The preceding conclusion was based upon a single datum. More abundant evidence meets us when we come to the study of King Lear's most perfect character. Those about Kent profess at one time or another their faith in an all-just Providence; Kent is silent. He finds himself in the stocks. "Fortune, good night: smile Lear II. ii. 180. once more; turn thy wheel!" is his comment. As we proceed, we discover that his "fortune" is the very negation of Providence. For if, in the phrase, "If fortune brag V. iii. 280. of two she loved and hated," you re-

[1] If the position taken in the text is correct, the duke in this passage must be understood as talking after the manner of the people. However, even if it could be shown that he believed nothing but fear of eternal punishment could restrain a criminal nature, it would not follow that he believed in the reality of such punishment. In Act II., scene iii., ll. 30-34, he is plainly speaking in his character as confessor. This attitude towards wrongdoing nowhere recurs in his lines.

place "fortune" by God, you get what is little short of blasphemy. Our last sight of Kent is when he comes to bid his king and master aye good-night. If "aye" means anything, **V. iii. 234.**
he is expecting a sleep that has no to-morrow's waking. After all, there is to be no farewell between them; Lear is beyond that. When the last breath has left the weary body, Kent knows it is well with the old king. He is no longer stretched upon the rack of this tough world. But not a word falls from Kent's lips of a better land in which we shall meet with a recompense for our afflictions.

Most of these facts have been noticed before; but one circumstance has as yet, so far as I know, entirely escaped attention. Kent was not always an unbeliever. At the beginning of the play, when he is still one that fortune loves, he addresses his master:

> "Royal Lear,
> Whom I have ever honour'd as my king,
> Loved as my father, as my master fol-
> low'd, **I. i. 141.**
> As my great patron thought on in my
> prayers."

This is no mere conventional mode of speech, like "the gods reward your kindness!" **III. vi. 5.**
or "God bless you." It is part of a solemn conjuration in which every word is intended to have its full value. Moreover, the prayers Kent

addressed to heaven, were no mere form. He is too honest, too single-minded, and too blunt to trifle with religious observances that mean nothing to him. Finally, one who could step between Lear's safety and his formidable wrath does not pray in order to be seen of men. Nor can the appearance of this expression be set down to accident. I know the casual reader of the plays will smile at this statement; but there are no accidents in the great tragedies. Least of all in King Lear. In the compass of thirty-two hundred lines is told a story almost as full of incident as War and Peace, crowded with characters as clearly conceived and as completely developed as those of the Russian novel. These wonderful results are accomplished by an employment of suggestion that has no parallel in literature. The effect of every word is carefully measured; it always reveals something; it may reveal much. What, then, is inferable from this innocent-looking phrase? As a prosperous nobleman, Kent has never had any occasion to doubt the existence of Providence. Evil he must have seen, but he has never known, or at any rate realized, its worst possibilities. Then comes overwhelming misfortune to one he loves, coupled with the revelation of malignant wickedness in those whom he has personally known. As a result, God has gone from his world. The sufferings and the heartlessness in his master's family cost him not only his life, but also his religious faith.

Three or four years pass, and then, if a plausible

chronology be correct, appears a series of romantic dramas which practically close Shakespeare's career as an author. They are Pericles, Cymbeline, The Winter's Tale, and The Tempest. In these, especially in the first three, there is noticeable a great alteration in tone. Now, when suspicion casts its shadow over an innocent life, the vital forces are preserved from blight by faith in powers divine, through whom

> "Innocence shall make
> False accusation blush and tyranny
> Tremble at patience." **W. T. III. ii. 31.**

When men are led to good by devious paths whose end, as they walked, could not be seen, they confess it is the gods

> "That have chalk'd forth the way
> Which brought us hither." **Tempest V. i. 203.**

The human instrument of deliverance from evil is a minister of God. Gratitude for protecting care, submission under affliction as "a punishment or trial," are the uniform attitude in either extremity of fortune. The passages cited are not isolated utterances, acceptable to some, repudiated by others. They represent the atmosphere in which all these men and women habitually live. **Pericles V. iii. 59–63. Pericles V. i. 200–201; Cym. V. v. 476–8. Cym. III. vi. 11; W. T. V. i. 171–174.**

Our investigation thus shows us that the representative figures of Shakespeare's dramas are neither exclusively believers in a providential order nor exclusively skeptics. We discover, moreover, that if we arrange his works in their probable chronological order, the metaphysical beliefs of these selected characters arrange themselves in a kind of Hegelian spiral. We pass from naïve, unmediated confidence, through doubt, to a certainty that has included and overcome its skepticism.

What more natural than to infer from these facts the course of Shakespeare's own religious history? As a man of thirty-five his mind is illumined, warmed, and vivified by a spontaneous, vigorous trust in God. Then, as the meaning and extent of human suffering and wickedness are revealed, there arise questionings, then doubts, then denial. His mind, like his works, is shrouded in gloom, a gloom pierced by no ray of light from a higher world. Finally comes deliverance. He reconquers the faith of his youth, though he holds it with a different spirit. Evil he now recognizes as a fact, but he sees in part, at least, how it can form an element in a divine plan. Justice and love rule the world, and we may believe they do all things well.

Plausible as this inference from the work to the architect may seem, I cannot think we ought to allow ourselves to accept it. The structure of conjecture is too large and heavy for the slight foundation of indisputable fact which is the best it is possible to supply. In interpreting the plays themselves we may be less rigorous. Each of them is a group of problems or puzzles, set for the spectator's pleasure and profit. The answers lie deep where the superficial and the indolent shall never find them. They will take Lady Macbeth's words, he "is too full o' the milk of human kind- **Macbeth I. v. 18.** ness to catch the nearest way," as the key to Macbeth's character. They will innocently believe that seasoned liar, the Duke of Vienna, when he tells Friar Thomas he is dis- **M. for M. I. iii. 19–54.** guising himself merely to watch the enforcement of an unpopular law. No, the dramatist is subtle and will let no one win the prize who is not willing to observe carefully, to think patiently, — and to pay for more than one ticket of admission. But it lies in the very nature of the game that the solution must not be beyond the reach of human ingenuity. We must have data in sufficient number, and none of them, when viewed in its proper relation to the rest, ought to be misleading. Therefore, in a properly constructed drama the most probable explanation of an action or character, even if it be only barely probable, is the true one. This holds even where the number of our data is ridiculously small, for we must believe we were given all we need.

Not so in life. Nature has entered into no tacit agreement with us to preserve all that is required for the answers to our questions, and to provide a corrective for misleading facts. Hence the vanity of most attempts, considering the paucity of our data, to worm the secrets of

Shakespeare's life out of his written works. I do not claim that the plays reveal absolutely nothing about the mind and the experience which were their source; here and there we may undoubtedly detect the man in the pattern he is weaving. But I do maintain that the material brought together in the preceding paragraphs, or the material as yet presented by any other student of Shakespeare, is totally inadequate for the construction of a theory of his positive theological beliefs.

Quite apart from this general ground for suspending judgment, the facts we have been passing in review are susceptible of more than one explanation. Even if they constrained us — as they do not — to the conclusion that at different periods the dramatist was specially interested in some one of the various phases of religious belief, a considerable number of grounds for such interest could easily be suggested. Among these, acceptance, whether in part or whole, of the creed delineated can hardly urge an exceptional claim. Our prolegomena, at least in so far as Shakespeare is concerned, must therefore close with a profession of ignorance.

This secret we may never hope to pierce. But the poet's thought about the relation of belief in a providential order to the tasks and problems of every-day life he has recorded where all may read. He has shown, over and over again, the power of such belief to comfort, sustain, and strengthen the soul in its conflict with calamity, passion, and public wrong. He has also affirmed with equal distinctness the possibility of living and conquering without it. There are men even to-day who are not ashamed to proclaim from the housetops their unwillingness to fight the good fight until assured of being on the winning side. In inspiring contrast to them stand certain of Shakespeare's characters who, cheered by no sure faith either in personal reward or the ultimate triumph of the good cause, deliberately range themselves on the side of right, and hold their allegiance in defeat as in victory. "Victrix causa diis placuit, sed victa Catoni." "The gods took the side of the victorious cause, but Cato the side of the vanquished." This is the temper in which Brutus and Kent fought, endured, and died.

Such men, Shakespeare saw, are facts. He was, furthermore, convinced that their judgments of value would still remain sound, the ends they pursued worth attaining, even if the universe should turn out to be nothing better than a lifeless machine. For if his tragedies are studies in failure, failure does not consist for him, as it does and must for Dante and Bunyan, in losing the chance of heaven, whether through the omission of some rite, through entanglement in a plausible heresy, or through death in the midst of unrepented and unexpiated sin. Just as little does it consist in disobedience to a supersensible law, or failure to prepare for some higher mode of existence. The tragedy of life, in his eyes, is that men do not know how to gain the best in life itself, or that knowing, they have not the power to guide will by insight, or that knowing and willing, they may be cut off from attainment by forces beyond their art to control. Such an attitude is not incompatible with beliefs and aspirations that pierce the senses' tenuous veil. But it gives the lie alike to the theology of Tridentine priest and Genevan theocrat. Furthermore, it could never coexist with the dogma unweariedly proclaimed, that where man possesses no metaphysical creed his interest in the passing show of things is an illusion, and his morality a parasite.

"Our days are few; therefore, let us make the most of them," wrote the imperial sage, Marcus Aurelius. "Our days are few. Emptied of transcendental significance, they are vain and worthless; let us throw them away," cries the Kantian philosophy. The former is the creed of Shakespeare, as of Shakespeare's heroes.

> "The time of life is short!
> To spend that shortness basely were too long,
> If life did ride upon a dial's point,
> Still ending at the arrival of an hour."

1 Henry IV. V. ii. 82.

A call to action this; a message of cheer and courage to an age that sees the old theology vanishing into air and knows not yet what the new shall be.

INDEX